This third and final part of poet, novelist and art critic Vinod Bhardwaj's trilogy (which began with Seppuku and was followed by A True Lie, the latter a depiction of the decline of journalism) looks at the massive downturn faced by the Indian art market post-2008 and the negative impact of notebandi from an unusual, almost surreal viewpoint. The novel's protagonist, Jai Kumar, is the son of a postman born in the middle of the blood-soaked times of Delhi's notorious Sikh massacre of 1984. The fleeting taste of the fruits of the sudden spurt in the Indian art market during 2004-2007 leaves Jai Kumar's creative instincts stunted. He now begins to look upon himself as a sex addict while the new surrealist grammar of the art bazaar strengthens this illusion of his sex life being a mark of sickness.

Delhi's art world also has an underground stream and as an art critic Vinod Bhardwaj has known it from close quarters. Artists have often related to him anecdotes about someone harbouring the illusion of being a sex addict and these have come handy in weaving the episodes in this novel. Sometimes the real is far more surreal than the imaginary. The bitter truth about India's changing political landscape also forms the background of the novel. And central to it are characters who tend to interpret the dramatic decline in the art market in 2008 in the light of the decline in the fortunes of the Congress. They had pinned their hopes on Narendra Modi's economic policies but became disillusioned in no time. Is Jai Kumar able to save his true passion for art in this scenario? Is he sick or the society and the politics around him?

Brij Sharma was born in 1949 in Laksar, Uttarakhand, where his father was a railway guard. After a desultory education in Dehra Dun in schools for the underprivileged, he joined the Times of India as a trainee journalist in 1973 as a batchmate of Vinod Bhardwaj. Six years later, soon after his return from a fellowship in West Germany, he left for the Gulf to waste 11 years with Khaleej Times in Dubai. He has also translated Vinod Bhardwaj's first two parts of this trilogy into English, co-edited with him two F N Souza exhibition catalogues, and edited the autobiography of Jack Gibson, the last English principal of Mayo College in Ajmer, which was published from the US. He has also translated into English Indian artist Ram Kumar's Europe Ke Sketch published in his youth which is forthcoming from Pundole Gallery in Mumbai.

He was Editor of Indian Express in Gujarat in the early 1990s and subsequently worked as a journalist in Bahrain until his return to India in 2019. He now lives between Goa and Dehradun.

THE DIARY OF A SEX ADDICT

VINOD BHARDWAJ

Translated from Hindi by

Brij Sharma

YATRA BOOKS
An imprint of Vani Prakashan Group

Peparback Edition : 2023

vaniprakashan.com

Yatra Books is an imprint of Vani Prakashan Group

Head Office

4695, 21-A, Daryaganj, New Delhi 110 002, India
Phone : +91 11 23273167, 23275710

Registered Bookstores and Offices

Ashok Rajpath, Patna-800 004, Bihar
Coffee House Campus, Mahatma Gandhi Marg, Allahabad-211 001, Uttar Pradesh
Mahatma Gandhi International Hindi University, Wardha-442 001, Maharashtra
36-A, Shakespeare Sarani, Near Rani Birla Girls College, Kolkata-700017, West Bengal

sales@vaniprakashan.in
vaniprakashan@gmail.com

The Diary of a Sex Addict
by Vinod Bhardwaj
Translated from Hindi by Brij Sharma

ISBN : 978-93-5775-275-6
Non-Fiction

Price : ` 295

Printed and bound in India at IBH Print & Bind Pvt. Ltd.

Dedication

To those 'discerning' readers who often mistake a realistic portrayal of sex as pornography. This novelist, though, considers the brutal realities of the contemporary art market as the actual pornographic reality.

Contents

Chapter 1

THE SOB STORY OF AN UNDIES

Some days are grand, some are gentlemanly, and there are days which can be called rogue.

But can days really be rogue? There certainly are wretched days but I prefer to call them rogue.

18 September 2008 was one of those rogue days. I looked at the morning paper which had this picture of a party where I stood in the middle, but the caption given by the good-for-nothing foolish subeditor read: 'Famous painter Pankaj Kumar with a friend.' How come this two-penny subeditor didn't know me? I picked up the phone and contacted the magazine's editor Radhika. "Madam, what's happening in your paper?"

Radhika hadn't yet got out of bed. "Why are you phoning to bore me in the early morning Mr Next Subodh Gupta?" she said, "Let me sleep in peace. I was in the office till late into the night but unlike yours, my nights are not spent hopping parties and having fun."

I flung the phone away. Now it was that worthless painter Pankaj Kumar's turn to phone me. "Boss, things have really gone out of hand. How come the photographer didn't know you? Did you forget to thrust a hundred-rupee note into his pocket?"

"Listen you dumb-ass, you can gloat the whole day. I guess you pushed a 500-note into his pocket for not identifying me in the caption."

But it looked like the rogue day still had some surprises in store for me. I had to go to Gallery Kuber to see its director Mrs Kasliwal. The appointment was for 11 in the morning but my girlfriend Shobha had lost her cool, packed her bag and left fuming on noticing a packet of condoms in my bag.

"You are telling me that you have some important work to do. You haven't even had your breakfast. Because your real work is dalliance with Mrs Kasliwal. You bloody cheat. Bloody sex addict. I don't want to put up in your studio."

Shobha was livid. She called a taxi and left. Then Mrs Kasliwal gave me a third jolt of the day. "Mr Jai Kumar, I'm sorry. The gallery is compelled to terminate your contract. In the last six months not even one work of yours has sold."

The termination of the contract meant a huge loss of half a million rupees every month. Mrs Kasliwal was in a hurry to go somewhere. Her driver was waiting so she quickly got into hercar.

But in a fit of anger, I planted myself in front of her car. "Don't behave like a kid, Jai. Get out of the way."

But I stood my ground for some good five minutes. It's only when I noticed the gallery guard approaching that I thought it prudent to leave the scene. By this time the entire gallery staff was watching the fun.

It was indeed a bloody rogue day. I returned to my studio and rang up Ramesh Gulati, my friend in Holland. He'd been a close friend in my college days, had subsequently left India and was now settled down in The Hague. Only recently I had revived my association with him on Facebook. He had asked me many times to visit his 'humble abode'. "I know you are now a star but see if you can come down to spend a few days in the studio of this forgotten star. I can guarantee you won't get bored."

Some months ago, I had obtained a one-year Schengen visa courtesy the Italian Embassy. I told my travel agent to book a ticket for the morning of 19 September. The flight was empty.

"Gulati dear, I have been thinking about you all day. Come to the airport tomorrow morning. Your friend is arriving. I know you are very fond of pickles. I will try to hoodwink the customs. And yes, you are also very fond of *kaju barfi* so I've ordered a one-kilo box of that as well."

My flight landed in Amsterdam in the early morning. Gulati was a changed man I noticed. The long hair was gone and he had turned nearly bald. I was moved by his Punjabi *jhappi* style of greeting me. Especially since at the moment I was suffering from depression and low esteem.

Gulati put my suitcase in an old, secondhand car and it dawned on me that I had had certain misgivings about him. He was no better than an illegal Punjabi immigrant arriving in Europe in search of employment. I also learnt that even his doddering vehicle belonged to some friend of his working at the Indian Embassy.

Gulati had been living in The Hague for the last eight years. In the beginning he did manage to sell some of his works, made some money and even bought a house. But for the last three or four years he'd been living on the edge. "Arre, now some artists here tell me that the art market in India is in a better shape. They even ask me to organise their shows there."

"Until last year the art market there was bounding. If you had visited India at that time, I would have made sure every work of yours was sold. People were landing up with bagsful of cash to pick up paintings in those days. Wonder where they have disappeared all of a sudden."

Gulati had a tiny house. To make ends meet, he had rented out one room in the back to some illegal Punjabi workers. There were five boys occupying that room.

I became a little worried. "You have quite a crowd in your studio. I think I'll have to join a queue even to visit the toilet I guess."

"Don't worry *yaar*. Two of the unfortunates leave for work at 3 in the morning and by 7 you won't find anybody here. On Sundays they are busy at the *langar* in the local gurudwara."

Gulati was also preparing to leave. He had a part-time job as a courier which brought in a little bit of cash.

"Listen, why don't you come over to Delhi. This is hardly the life for a painter here."

Gulati smiled a wan smile. "Delhi is a bigger hell for a struggling painter. At least here you can easily have some basic comforts of life. You do a bit of hard work, have beer and enjoy the girls."

And he left home with his courier bag. In college days I would be jealous when I looked at his paintings. He had now probably forgotten all about painting.

The Punjabi boys were very amiable. They would be through with their morning rituals hurriedly and then disappear. Occasionally they would cook chicken or mutton at night when Gulati and me were invariably invited to join them. The very first evening I found Gulati quite enjoying their company. He hardly bore any resemblance to a painter. After downing a couple of pegs he even started to sing and dance.

I was getting bored. Inside the toilet, on every side, the boys had pasted raunchy posters of Dutch girls in the nude. When I went in to pee, I felt relieved only after masturbating. And damn it, who was the one whose name I recalled towards the end? No, it was not Shobha, it was Mrs Kasliwal. In my fantasy I was masturbating standing in front of her car. And her driver was looking at me with his eyes popping out.

Gulati was free until the following afternoon. He had borrowed his Embassy friend's car for a week to take me round. He decided to take me to the seaside. It was quite windy but I had my inner wear, jacket, cap and muffler on. The strong winds would time and again blow away my cap, but I quite enjoyed it. After July the Delhi weather was spoilt by the advent of dengue and other ailments and therefore October, supposedly a fine-weather month, had now become the time to fight the ailments.

"You should have fallen in love with a wealthy Dutch girl instead of remaining a bachelor and getting bored," I said.

"There's no dearth of girls here. When I had had just arrived here, in the lane downstairs the hookers and call girls would be busy from morning till late in the night, openly inviting any one passing by for a 'suck and fuck'. They charged just 30 euros for a 20-minute service. So where was the need to fall in love? Love and everything else in that line are all rubbish. I gave up on love in the Hauz Rani lane in Delhi itself. Wonder where will Begum Ayesha be now? Perhaps towing her gaggle of half a dozen kids. She was beautiful though and loved me no end. The last I saw her was in Dr Bountra's clinic. She looked quite sick. Her children too appeared to be sick. Bountra was making good money in his lucrative business and was thinking of buying a new house.

"*Yaar* Gulati, you switch gears suddenly. Come, take me too to the world of 'suck and fuck'. I gather everything is safe here?"

At 11 in the morning the lane wore a deserted look. "It's crowded only at night," Gulati said. Before we entered the lane, he pointed to a villa across the road which was once occupied by Spinoza, the Dutch philosopher of Portuguese descent.

Gulati was counted among the most well-read persons in the college. He was quite well up on philosophy, history, etc. Right at the entrance of the lane, even as I was in the middle of taking in a black beauty behind a glass box, oblivious to my distraction, Gulati was busy edifying me: "Do you know about Spinoza's ideas? If a triangle could speak it would proclaim that God was triangular in all His majesty. Similarly, if a circle could speak it would declare God was circular. Which means everyone would endow God with his own identity and declare all the rest as clumsy."

"Which means this prostitute also would see God as a prostitute."

"Of course."

After I had taken a round of the lane, I felt disappointed.

"So? You didn't fancy anyone?"

"They are all worthless. Such drained bodies."

"Come, I'll take you to a lane near the railway station. It's a little upmarket where you'll have to shell out 50 euros. But you'll find a good choice."

We decided to walk up to the lane. By now Gulati had switched over to Sartre from Spinoza and we were discussing 'nothingness'.

This lane was certainly beautiful and inviting. A girl wearing specs and flaunting the look of an intellectual sat there holding a book.

I pushed Gulati ahead since he knew workable Dutch. But the girl turned her face away. "Listen, this is patently insulting. She seems to be a racist."

"No. It's not that. They also like to choose for themselves. After all they also have a right to say 'no.'"

I fancied a tall blonde who appeared to be 30 something and looked quite glamorous in her bra and panty. But by then I had moved on and reached the next cabin where a dusky girl was trying all her tricks to attract me. She was lovely too, but the blonde had totally ensnared me.

"You have moved on so now you have to walk the full circle to once again arrive in front of the blonde."

"What if she rejects me?"

"No problem. There are so many other girls. We are quite close to the railway station."

"But that blonde girl is okay."

"Here you'll find college students, practising engineers, even a wealthy farmer's wife. They book their cabins online and don't look at what they do here as something to be ashamed of. It's not like the notorious Sonagachhi area of Kolkata."

"Why are you conferring so much respect on this profession? It's the same everywhere."

The blonde beauty understood English. She slowly opened the glass door which meant I was allowed to step in. I took 50 euros out of my bag and handed her and then entrusted my iPad and bag to Gulati.

"You have just 20 minutes. I'll wait for you outside."

Only 20 minutes! It would take 10 minutes to take off my clothes alone. I had put on clothes like the layers of onion skin. The blonde beauty quickly got rid of her undies and bra and sat down on the bed, waiting for me.

I was nervous. Also, a bit diffident. The blonde was beautiful and spoke very softly.

I hesitated for a time but then had to spew it: "I want to go to the loo to release my bladder. It's quite cold and windy outside."

She pointed in the direction of the wash basin and said: "You can relieve yourself there."

Relieve myself into a wash basin? I was in a fix. There was a bidet next to the bed but that was for her exclusive use. I recalled an incident narrated in a column by Khushwant Singh where a Sardarji mistook a prostitute's bidet for a toilet seat and used it for a shit and was given a thrashing of his life by the hooker.

Anyway, I managed to use the wash basin to relieve myself. Then slowly took off my clothes even as the blonde watched me with curious eyes.

I now stretched myself on the bed naked. Part One of 'Suck and Fuck' was in progress. I now had only eight minutes.

But an artist's brain is full of fancies. I began to weigh 'Plan Quick Fuck'. I knew that she knew English, so I told her: "You fling all the Dutch expletives at me. And I'll retaliate in Hindi." She was totally in a mood to cooperate. So in the next eight minutes there was an uninterrupted bilingual exchange of expletives. I don't use expletives in my day-to-day dealings but if another driver's misconduct on the road arouses my anger then I can't help it. Beyond this, if a sophisticated and highly educated woman or girl is in bed with me then the use of choice forbidden words creates a kind of magical eroticism. When an intellectual beauty, in the heat of passion, invitingly asks me: 'Come on, fuck me', then I feel fulfilled. My sexual passion is roused manifold. I go mad as if in the throes of a 105-degree fever.

After that unusual sexual encounter all my frustrations, depression and sadness vanished without trace. I had travelled from sex to a state of meditation.

The blonde beauty gave me 'extra time' to put on my clothes. I also learnt she had booked the cabin for ten days. I was excited: "I'd like to come again tomorrow. You have thoroughly discharged all my depression. What a session of expletives."

But finally, I never revisited her. When I told Gulati about the session he slapped me on the shoulder and began to call me names in pure Punjabi. I did have a mind to revisit her and one day even went up to that lane all alone but then something made me change my mind and I returned to Gulati's rooms.

The birthday party of one of the Punjabi workers was in full swing. With songs and dance and chicken and Scotch, Gulati was in his true form.

I went into the toilet and in the middle of fixing my gaze on the raunchy posters of Dutch girls made the supreme donation of semen costing '80 euros per gram'. There was a time when it was claimed that semen was something so costly it could be priced 80 rupees per gram. But in Holland its price could only be counted in euros.

The following day I was at the Van Gogh Museum. I still had a day in hand for 'The Night Watch'. That day was reserved. I have great admiration for Rembrandt and I sat in the Rijks Museum for hours contemplating it. A new kind of energy was giving me strength. To hell with the art market. I'd paint what I want to paint. To hell with Mrs Kasliwal.

With the 'The Night Watch' before me, I recalled the day when, as I sat in her airconditioned limo on my first meeting with her, I told her without a moment's hesitation: "I'm sure the brand of your underwear is Victoria's Secret."

"Make a guess. It's named after your favourite painter."

"Souza Lingerie?"

"Taline Souza," she smiled.

I whispered into her ear: "Can you take off your undies and give it to me?"

"Why? What would you do with it? Would you go to sleep wearing it?"

"No. I'd keep it under my pillow before going to bed. Its scent will take me into the forests of sleep."

Hearing this, in one flick Mrs Kasliwal took off her undies from under her sari and quickly thrust it into my bag. Her driver could make out nothing.

I looked at the bag closely. Then continued to sniff it closely for a long while.

The Gallery Kuber contract was normally given only to eminent and senior artists. But Mrs Kasliwal gave one to a young painter like me which was a major achievement. I made a painting and quite skilfully incorporated that underwear in it and named the work 'Night Watch'.

Mrs Kasliwal got to see the painting only on the inaugural day of my show. Before she saw it, the work had already bowled over Anand Kasliwal, owner of the city's leading travel agency. Indeed, he was in the middle of getting himself photographed with the painting when Mrs Kasliwal dragged me to a corner. "What the hell are you doing Jai? Have you given it a thought?"

"Why? What happened Madam? Your husband has quite liked the work."

"What do you think? Won't he recognise my underwear? He is not colour blind. He had gifted it to me on Valentine's Day."

"I don't think he has recognised it. And why are you getting so worked up about an underwear?"

By now Anand Kasliwal had walked up to us and told his wife: "Please put a red sticker on this painting. It'll hang in my office." Mrs Kasliwal looked askance at her husband.

"Don't you see darling? Jai also fancies the same underwear which I had gifted to you. What a grand composition." Mrs Kasliwal was unable to make out whether her husband was mocking her or was really unable to realise the truth. I found it prudent to remain silent.

Then one of her husband's friends arrived and began to comment on the painting in minute detail. Mrs Kasliwal now told me in high dudgeon: "Listen, I'd give you the matching bra as well. You better incorporate that too in the painting. It'll make a good triptych."

At that point I started to search for a glass of wine. And Mrs Kasliwal scurried away towards the mall so she could show her husband the underwear of the same colour and design lying safely with her.

In the light of the red wine I now began to chat with art critic Mathur. That was another torture.

Chapter 2

'F' PAINTING

I was born in November 1984 in the Malviya Nagar area of Delhi in a rented house located in a lane occupied mostly by Sikhs. My mother would tell me that I had announced the good [or bad] news of my arrival in the middle of the blood-soaked times that befell Delhi in the aftermath of Indira Gandhi's assassination. My art guru Francis Newton Souza was born 60 years before me i. e. in 1924 in Goa.

My father was a postman. A humble soul and a man of very few words. During my childhood I would found him busy and happy only around Diwali. My mother had a tailoring machine and added to the family income by sewing clothes from home. I also had a sister who was seven years my senior.

My mother's family lived in Bahalpur, a village in Punjab, and we'd visit it every summer during vacations. Sometimes father would turn up there but only to fetch us. I began to make drawings from an early age. When I was 15, one day I noticed my guru Souza in the Dhoomimal Art Gallery in the company of a very young woman. I stepped forward on an impulse to touch his feet but he quickly withdrew. Then I showed him my sketchbook and got a pat on the back. On that day I put up a picture of Souza in my room which till now hangs in my studio. I always have this feeling Souza is looking down on me. When I am in the middle of making a painting, I do have this habit of looking at his picture every now and then. If the mood to have sex in the studio grips me the first thing I do is take the picture down and place it on the floor, face down. Though Gulati would say: "Souza Baba would have been only too happy to see you in the middle of enjoying sex. He himself watched blue films right up to his old age."

Since my mother ran this smalltime tailoring business, the Sikh girls and women in the neighbourhood would come to her regularly. I quite fancied one aof them. Her name was Kulwant Kaur. She was fair-complexioned, quite cool and sexy. One day, when I was eight, I was tormented by an unbearable headache. Kulwant Kaur noticed me and said: "Come on *beta*, let me massage your scalp with some almond oil." Mother too chipped in: "Yes *beta*, auntie will shoo away your headache in no time."

Kulwant Kaur trapped me between her thighs quite viciously and then massaged my scalp with all the love she could muster. I wondered if her intent also was to have her own thighs massaged. At the age of 14, while on summer vacations in Bahalpur, I headed for a field of watermelons at high noon and masturbated for the first time. And offered the libation of my first ejaculation to Kulwant Kaur with sincere devotion and humility. I still have numerous drawings of Kulwant Kaur in my sketchbook. In those days I would try to draw nudes in Souza's style. When I was in the 10th std, my sister discovered the sketchbook one day and immediately recognised Kulwant Kaur. Then said: "Shall I tell Ma that you draw Auntie's dirty pictures?"

"Who says they are dirty pictures? Fine, go and tell Ma. I'm not afraid. Then I'd also show Ma the letters that our neighbour Surjit writes to you."

"You know I don't fancy bearded guys. I tear up that loafer's letters there and then and throw them away."

When I was growing up to be a strapping young man, my first girlfriend Jaswinder, carried away in the middle of a stormy embrace, confided in me: "Your sister told me that once she had secretly watched you spilling your sperm."

Today I look upon myself as a sex addict but am I really one? Was Souza a sex addict? In my college days I had once asked Gulati: "Listen, tell me if you know of a sex doctor. I have many questions for him."

"Why? I am a sex doctor myself. You can ask me whatever you want. Do you want to know anything about *saande ka tel*?"

Quite naturally, my father did not want me to spoil my life by going to an arts college. He looked upon the artist fraternity itself as lowborn.

When I was in my second year in the college my father died in a road accident while on the way to drop letters and parcels on his bicycle. That scene still leaves me traumatised – my father's body covered in cuts and bruises lying in the middle of letters strewn all over. Though he didn't like the fact that I had chosen the path of art he was a noble human being.

He was rather thin and scrawny. One day mother handed me his shirts and said: "You might like to wear them. They're new and the right size for you."

For the annual exhibition at my college I had done a poignant painting about my late father's shirt. It showed both me and him in the same shirt. The painting won a prize and a gallery even bought it. In 2005, by which time I had become a young painter with some notoriety, that painting was sold at an auction at a record-breaking price. I had also placed a bid to get the painting back but my postman father's simple and cheap shirt turned out to be quite a pricey lot.

By the way that shirt is still lying in my wardrobe. And I do wear it on special occasions. I never liked my father's image of a postman going about on a bicycle – perhaps even hated it. But I developed a sort of mysterious affection for his shirt.

The stray dogs around the Sikh lane were a big problem for me. When I was seven, a ferocious dog bit my bottom hard and ran away. But instead of taking me for a course of injections my mother would go about gathering the latest information about that dog to ensure it was all right and hadn't turned mad. And it could certainly be seen roaming around in fine fettle.

Another time, when I was around 19, a dog bit me in the dark and vanished. This time I went to the doctor on my own and completed the course of injections. When I finally left that lane, I felt the dogs would henceforth spare me.

But now dogs began to attack me even on the eve of my foreign jaunts. When I was on my way to Paris in 2006, a dog chose to bite me. This time it was a posh colony in south Delhi – Defence Colony. Mercifully I had enough time to complete the course of injections before my departure.

Then in 2008 when I was on my way to Madrid to see Picasso's *Guernica*, just a day before my departure, as I was stepping out of a chemist's shop, I came in the way of a playful scrape between two dogs. Then I noticed my bleeding leg where the sharp teeth of one of the canines had grazed the skin. The doctor cautioned me that in case of rabies I would not escape death which could be quite horrific and that it was necessary to complete the course of injections. I took the first injection in Delhi and figured that since there was no shortage of dogs in Europe I should be able to easily complete the course there.

So on my first day in Madrid, instead of heading to see *Guernica* I was busy looking for the rabies injection at the chemists. Finally, I learnt that Spain was a rabies-free nation and therefore no chemist stocked the injections. I then went to a hospital where a team of doctors struggling against the language barrier somehow conveyed to me that quite a distance away from the city centre there was indeed a place where the injections might be available and I could find some help.

I somehow managed to reach that centre the following day. It was a place where the students leaving for other countries were administered all manner of injections. There was a tiny room in a corner occupied by a short-statured doctor who was the rabies expert. She also knew English and that's how I finally found the facility to have the rabies injections administered to me.

I asked the doctor: "Why are dogs always after me? In Delhi every residential area has a full-fledged army of stray dogs."

"Maybe they are attracted by your skin odour," she said with a smile.

On leaving the hospital I sat down on an empty bench in a lovely garden. There were any number of dogs around. But in Europe or America dogs are the pride of their owners.

I suddenly noticed a ferocious dog in the distance. It was running towards me and soon came quite close to where I sat. But its owner stopped it in its tracks by giving it some command from a distance and it meekly went back to her.

My visit to the doctor to take an injection in 2003 turned out to be a decisive moment in my life. I had gone to Dr Arun Bhargava for the injection.

He was a handsome doctor. Thirty something. "What do you do?" he asked.

"I'm a painter. Also studying at the Arts College."

"Do your paintings sell?"

"Yes, they are beginning to sell."

"My wife is also a painter. Her paintings don't really sell but she continues to paint relentlessly all the same. A wealthy friend of mine did buy two of her works just to please me and she bought a stack of art material with the money. Now she has rented a studio."

"I would certainly like to meet her."

Just then his wife Jyotsna walked into the clinic. She was a convent-educated woman, quite fluent in English, whereas I was a young painter who had studied in a municipal school. I was quite weak in English and was unable to interact with her initially. But soon enough she took off her English cover.

"If you have time to spare why don't you come over to my studio," she suggested. "I have done a lot of new work and your opinion could be useful for me. You see I am a self-made painter. Never went to any college to learn."

I looked at Dr Bhargava. He said: "I haven't been able to visit her studio yet. How can I? I hardly find time from my clinic."

Jyotsna drove her handsome limo herself. Her studio was on the third floor of a building in a narrow lane in Lado Sarai. We strode up negotiating a ramshackle stairscase. But everything was on a grand scale inside. There was also an air-conditioner, a kitchen, and a stock of beer in the fridge. When I looked at the art material, I wondered whether I should flick some of it.

I picked up a drawing sheet and quickly began to draw Jyotsna's portrait. I was an expert in portraiture. She sat there completely astonished as she contemplated the result.

"How much? What's the price?"

"It's free for you."

"No, I don't accept anything for free."

"Fine. The price is a large can of beer."

Jyotsna took out two cans from the fridge, then offered me a cigarette. I declined since I don't smoke but she lit one for herself. Then she switched the music system on. The magical strains of 'Bolero' were having a strangely delirious effect on me.

"Was it your love marriage with Doctor Bhargava?"

"No. An arranged one. My mother knew his family for many years."

"I found Dr Bhargava to be a thorough gentleman."

"No doubt. He *is* a gentleman. But I am unfit for gentlemen. I like naughty men like you."

"Do I look naughty?"

"You are a complete rogue. Women manage to check out a man in one glance."

"But you appear to be a gentlewoman to me."

She burst out laughing. "I'm a rogue of the first order."

I heard her in silence and continued to look at the dry patches of paint on the floor. It was a completely chaotic and wild studio. The tubes of colours strewn all over added to the anarchic atmosphere. Though even I do not like squeaky clean studios.

I had once gone to see Manjit Bawa in his Garhi studio. I found it wasn't all that clean or organised when he said: "After I have done for the day I always clean my brushes with water and keep them in a perfect state." And I watched him mesmerised for a long time as he sat cleaning his brushes.

"Where are you lost Mr Young Man," Jyotsna asked as she took out another cigarette.

"Have you ever exhibited your works?"

"No. But I do mean to hold a big show. It will be called 'F Painting'.

"F? You mean Fine?"

She laughed. "No. Fuck Painting. There are those who paint holding the brush in the mouth. And there are others who paint with fire. But I want to make fuck paintings."

"I don't follow you Madam."

"First of all, never again call me Madam. I hate this mode of address."

I looked at her in silence.

"I want someone to fuck me from behind and at that moment I should be frenetically painting on the canvas spread on the floor as I experience orgasm."

"Will Doctor Saheb agree for this unusual experiment?"

"What is this rant of Dr Saheb? You need to change yourself. The powerful lines of your portrait signal that you are going to be a great painter. Those who address people as Saheb and Madam can never aspire to be great painters."

Then she fell silent, finished the can of beer in one go and said: "I feel you can be a good companion for my fuck painting."

It was now becoming increasingly difficult for me to carry on with the façade of being a gentleman. The creative beast inside me had woken up by now and was desperate. I got up and spread the canvas on the floor and arranged the colours and brushes around it. Then spread a worn bedsheet on the floor and began to remove Jyotsna's clothes with all the tricks of a scoundrel. It was quite obvious she was enjoying all my dirty manoeuvres.

She was beautiful, sexy and not much older than me. I had this feeling a ferocious hunting dog was crouching inside me.

Jyotsna appeared to be painting in a frightening fury reminiscent of Jackson Pollock. I didn't want to discharge so early. I wanted to watch her paint for an extended period of time. I stopped my exertions for a moment.

"Don't stop damn it. My painting is close to being finished."

That day, as I slowly descended the stairs of Jyotsna's studio, I had this feeling a kind of strange angelic soul was following me.

"You didn't even give me your number. What kind of a friendship is this?" I barked back my number from the lane and she gave me a missed call.

I was to go to Dr Bhargava to complete the course of rabies injections but I couldn't muster the courage to visit his clinic. In any case the injections could be administered at any clinic on the basis of their schedule in the chart. I therefore zeroed in on a clinic run by a beautiful lady doctor.

Since there was no phone call from Jyotsna for a week, I began to forget that one-night stand [though one might also label it as one-afternoon stand] as a minor adventure.

Then suddenly, a leading agent of the art bazaar recognized my talent while I was still in college. When a dealer gave me a cheque for Rs 1.25 lac my mother began to cry: "How happy your father would be if he were here."

Remembering father's bicycle I had now begun to dream of owning a car. That Sikh lane seemed like a forgettable past.

But Jyotsna had not yet taken leave from my life. One day I got her call: "I was thinking you'd phone me one of these days. You didn't even come to the clinic for the injection. One must take the rabies injections on time."

She called me to her studio in the afternoon. It was redolent with the fragrance of flowers. She took off her clothes and began to put on the flowers like some kind of jewellery. The studio also had a small bedroom and she had strewn flowers on the bed there as well.

"You plan even a session of intercourse quite stylishly. Your husband must be left speechless."

She didn't say anything, just looked at me. Then said: "The husband thinks all this is a form of madness. For him having intercourse is as good as giving an injection. He seems to have left behind his imagination in some medical lab."

It struck me that a painting made in the middle of flowers in the course of an intercourse could also be called F Painting - Flower Painting.

"If your husband is so boring, why don't you leave him? How long are you going to put up with him?"

"I also have a a two-year-old daughter Neha. It's not all that easy to leave everything behind. And it's not all that easy for me to make a living through my paintings. For your information my husband doesn't pay this studio's rent. My mother, who is the head nurse in a hospital, pays both the rent and the expenses to buy the art material. My husband believes my passion is a form of useless expenditure."

I looked at Jyotsna and had this feeling I had known her for years.

"My daughter's birthday falls next week. Why don't you make a nice card for the party."

Sitting right there in the studio I designed a lovely and colourful card and Jyotsna was very pleased. "And yes, you have to come to the party."

"I'd be bored and it'd also be difficult to look your husband in the eye."

"No, you have to come. I'll send my car to pick you up. Neha should also be happy to see you. She'd also be very pleased to see this card."

But on Neha's birthday Jyotsna called in the morning: "Sorry Jai, my husband says the party is only for the family members and his friends. He had a cheque for two thousand rupees for you for making the card but I tore it up. Idiot."

"You are upset for no reason. I'd have got bored at the party in any case. We'd meet at the studio next week. Think of something new."

"Oh yes, next week I have to take out some old jewellery from the bank locker to attend a marriage. I have a fantastic idea in my mind."

"Do you mean to turn yourself into *Utsav*'s heroine Rekha?"

"No. Something beyond that."

My friendship with Jyotsna lasted three years. She had become my adventurous lover. Both of us would devise ever new ways of having an intercourse. Our props ranged from a palm tree to a running motorcycle.

Finally, Jyotsna's dream of becoming an artist did get realized. An entire hall at Taj Hotel was booked for the show which she named 'F Painting'. She entrusted the responsibility of Page 3 publicity to the capital's biggest PRO Meghna. A small Press conference was also organized before the show.

There was an unbelievably glamorous atmosphere at the show. Dr Bhargava gave me a hearty welcome. Jyotsna spoke to journalists dressed in an elegant sari.

"Madam, what is this F Painting? Is it a new experiment?"

"My entire show is a sort of experiment. The F in a painting can mean many things. Fine painting, Flower painting… there are many meanings…"

Then after a gap of silence she suddenly blurted: "It can also be a Fuck painting. Or a Fuck You painting. Or a Fuck Off painting."

The stunned and speechless journalists stood there staring at Jyotsna.

I now went up and planted myself near the work which was the real Fuck painting. I said to Jyotsna: "I want to buy it for my collection. Put a red sticker on it."

"No. It's not for sale. My husband likes it a lot. It hangs in our bedroom."

Through her first solo show Jyotsna managed to find what Andy Warhol called 15 minutes of fame.

I was quite disturbed by Jyotsna's one disgusting habit. She was always busy with temples, astrologers and tantriks. She would even drag me to many of them.

By now i. e. 2018 she has more or less given up painting. She no longer has a studio either. There is a notorious woman who goes by the name of Prabhuji among her followers. Lately Jyotsna has plunged herself into Prabhuji's world. The members of her group continue to meet among themselves.

She has taken a sort of premature retirement from the art world.

Chapter 3

ONE ART CRITIC AND TWO MICE

Mathur would often claim he was the only art critic of his generation to have completed a formal course for art curators in London. It was even printed on his visiting card. But there were people who whispered that the course was actually completed in Bhatinda. Nevertheless, I knew that Mathur had been to London many years ago and he had indeed attended some sort of a two-week crash course in art.

Speculations were rife even about Mathur's marital status. One version was that his wife lived in a village near Gorakhpur with his two daughters. Mathur even visited the village once on the occasion of his elder daughter's marriage. The other story doing the rounds was that his wife lived in Delhi itself, was an art teacher and had a daughter. But that one day, on stumbling upon some packets of condoms in Mathur's magic bag, she was so upset she moved to a rented house of her own. But Mathur has my full sympathy since I have gone through this experience myself.

Mathur himself claims to be a bachelor. In his tiny flat in Munirka there stands an almirah sandwiched between stacks of books and catalogues. Behind its glass panels one can notice the neatly arranged 20-volume set of an art encylopaedia resplendent in its golden binding. I guess one of the volumes may have been leafed through some five years ago. The lower shelves of this almirah are not visible from outside. But there are occasions when, if he is in an expansive mood after downing a peg or two, would unlock that section to show off his unrivalled collection of bottles of Scotch. A bottle of Blue Label can always be seen adorning the left corner. There are times when he would claim it was a gift from the German ambassador, on others that it was a birthday gift from a certain college principal who had a crush on him.

"What about offering me too something out of this magic corner. Are you sure what I see is not just an empty Blue Label box?"

One day Mathur got upset with my constant aspersions that took the bottle out and began to display it. "Touch it. It's the real stuff. I haven't even opened the seal."

Just then some girlfriend of his called up and he hurriedly left the room, glued to his mobile phone. This happened just as I was eyeing the half-empty bottle of single malt in another corner of the almirah. Mathur must be making pegs out of it in his moments of loneliness. I took it out and lost no time in downing two neat pegs. Then began to croon in the manner of Sunny Leone – 'Have two pegs and forget about them'.

Normally Mathur would never make this kind of mistake. My first impulse was to top up the shortfall by pouring some water into the bottle. He often complained that he suspected his maid helped herself on the sly with a shot of whisky from one of the open bottles and then topped it up with water. But I reckoned that trying to pour water into the bottle of single malt posed a bigger risk than stealing two pegs out of it.

It was only once that Mathur had gladly taken out a bottle of Black Dog from that locked-up section of the almirah and offered two pegs to me. That's another interesting story.

Two little mice had found their way into his house and were having a free run for four or five days. Mathur was dead scared of them and had specially phoned me and called me over so I'd help him find deliverance from the rowdy duo.

"Listen Jai Kumar. Please help me to get rid of these terrorists. I could hardly go to sleep last night."

"Every small and big artist in the capital fears you and here you are scared of these harmless mice?"

"You better come over right away. I have heard they sell something in the market which has a kind of glue all over and the mice get stuck on it. Bring it along and I'd pay."

"I'll come in the evening."

"Damn it, come fast otherwise I'll have to come over to you studio with a bag and sleep there."

"For your information a monstrous mouse makes at least one appearance in my studio every day. I always leave something for him to eat and he quietly finishes it and leaves. You might faint on seeing it. It's fearsome."

I was trying to imagine in what state would Mathur be at the other end considering he was already quite scared.

The Sikh lane where I had spent my childhood was in an area where it was quite common to find stray dogs in the street and wayward mice at home. At the very sight of a mouse I'd squash it in a flash with one flick of my rubber slippers.

I arrived at Mathur's at about 5 in the evening. On the way I had taken care to buy for 80 rupees a ludo-like glue strip to catch the mice.

Mathur actually looked a worried man. His mice would manage to get past even rat-traps. Actually, they were so small they would be moving in and out of the traps quite comfortably. The rascals won't touch the piece of bread. Someone had advised Mathur he should consider a rat-killing cake. The idea was that they would eat it and become so desperate with thirst that in their search for water they would run out of the house looking for an open space.

Mathur took courage, went to Bubbly's store in the neighbourhood and did buy some cake packets.

"I'm sure it works Bubbly. The mice have destroyed my sleep."

"Well, a lot of people buy them. I'm sure they work."

"Don't you have the glue strip?"

"No Mathur Saheb. You know I am a shopkeeper. Indeed, we worship mice. God knows how many of them are busy raising hell in my store at the back. But if you ask me, I've got used to them."

"Then why the hell do you sell these cakes?"

Bubbly was lost for words. "Mathur Saheb, actually my wife is quite disturbed that I sell them. But what to do. They are in great demand. Otherwise people would go to Agrawal's store who even stocks the glue strip." Mathur immediately rushed there but it was out of stock on that day.

On reaching home Mathur broke the cake into pieces and placed the bits in the kitchen and under the bookcase. An hour later he found that all the bits had disappeared. Which meant these had been eaten and by the evening the thirsty mice should be desperate to escape into the open. Mathur felt a bit relieved.

That night he reached home from a cocktail party rather late. There was no mice movement evident. He went to bed quite at peace with himself though was so drunk he couldn't even change into night clothes.

But when he went into the kitchen next morning to prepare tea, he found a mouse emerging from under the fridge. It seemed to be out on a morning walk quite naturally.

Just then a friend called up Mathur. After listening to his narrative steeped in sorrow his take was: "Mathur Saheb, you know better that the market is flooded with fake medicines. I'm sure your cakes too were fake."

Mathur flung into the air some choice expletives directed at Bubbly and then contacted me for help. By this time, he was almost grovelling. The agony of such an eminent art critic distressed me.

When I arrived at Mathur's carrying the ludo-like glue strip he actually presented a look of relief.

"Mathur Saheb, you better quit this ground-floor house and go to some 11th-floor flat. The mice would never be able to reach there."

"But Umesh, the painter who lives on the fifth floor, is also sick of mice. He told me they managed to reach his flat by climbing the pipes." Looked like Mathur had thoroughly researched the subject. He often claimed that I knew by heart the complete history of the red used by French painter Matisse. Evidently these days he was putting together all the latest information about mice.

As soon as I entered Mathur's house, I noticed a tiny and dirty-looking mouse scamper away into the kitchen. As I reached the kitchen it quickly slipped into a cupboard.

My father too was mortally afraid of mice. Whereas I'd squash one mercilessly and then pick it up by the tail and proudly take out the poor soul's funeral procession in full view of the lane's children.

I opened the cupboard, and as soon as the scared mouse jumped out, I ensured its salvation with my slipper in one second flat and picked it up by its tail to throw it in a garbage bin outside.

Mathur watched me with a scared look. "Yaar Jai Kumar, you have performed a miracle. You barely entered the house and sent one to heaven!"

On my return I found Mathur preparing two pegs of Black Dog with all the deference and respect he could muster. "Mathur Saheb, it's only 7 in the evening. Please wait a bit. Let me look for the second one."

"Arre yaar, today is a special day. You better presume that the sun is already set." The air conditioner and the Black Dog created quite an ambience in the middle of the smothering heat. Mathur now put on a movie on the DVD. It was titled *Shame*. Mathur was treating me like a very special guest.

"It's a very good film. You'd love it. It's hero is a sex addict exactly like you. I got it from London only last week."

"Sex addict? Who told you I'm a sex addict?" By now I had spied the second mouse out on a stroll behind the sofa across me. Next to it was the kitchen where I had squarely placed the glue strip. But the mouse steered clear of it and entered the kitchen. Clever bastard!

Mathur downed the first peg of Black Dog in one go. Then said: "Mrs Kasliwal gave me this information long ago. And what's there to be ashamed of in this? A number of big names in the art world have been sex addicts."

"That bitch is jealous of me. She cancelled my contract the moment the art market fell. That was long ago so let's leave it. Let's watch the movie. The mouse is looking for something in your kitchen."

"Did you see it enter?"

"Of course, went in avoiding the glue strip. It appears it's also an artful dodger like you."

"What do we do now?"

"Nothing. Just wait. It's bound to come out. The bastard is looking for meat in an eagle's nest. How can it find it?"

Mathur turned to me in frustration: "You are spinning a lot of yarns today. You know I am helpless."

"Anyway, Mathur Saheb, let's start the movie. I'm keeping an eye on the mouse."

I sat sipping the drink slowly. The film's hero even visits the office toilet to masturbate. He also finds it quite easy to have sex with a call girl. But when he takes a sexy and beautiful office colleague to a hotel, he finds himself sexually inadequate. And she leaves dissatisfied. The hero now contacts a call girl and manages to have sex with her quite easily. The problem begins when his sister also moves into his flat in New York. This starts to take toll on his private world of fantasy.

The film was good, but I was not like its protagonist. Whether it was a call girl or my girl friend or someone from a gallery or the distressed wife of a wealthy businessman – I always left them satisfied. Then why did this bloody Mathur call me a sex addict? I must quietly drop the live mouse inside his shirt. Only then would the bastard realize the truth.

The film had gripped me though I also had to keep an eye on the kitchen door. While the film's climax was in progress I suddenly noticed the mouse stuck to the strip. In its desperation to escape the strip it was getting stuck to it further.

Mathur immediately stopped the DVD. I picked up the strip with the mouse and went out to throw it in the garbage bin.

"Did you throw it into the bin right outside the house?"

"No Mathur Saheb. You have still to write the catalogue for my next exhibition. I threw it into the bin in the next block."

"Yaar, you are really great. You did me a big service today. Mrs Kasliwal is a stupid woman. I've also enjoyed her a lot and I believe she's a sex addict herself. You are still young, you have stamina, your art also has strength. Cheers!"

After leaving Mathur's house that evening I went for a stroll in the park nearby. I was thinking about my Italian friend Elisabetta. There was a time when I was madly in love with her. And she, 13 years my senior, was mad about an old and married Naxalite.

The situation in which I had seen the hero of *Shame* a while ago – helpless in front of an office colleague – had been my situation too in the face of Elisabetta once. When I recall that moment, I feel utterly ashamed of myself. I, who believed I was a Tarzan of sex, had to bite the dust in front of her. I have heard that even the Hindu *Purans* advise that it's a man's duty to satisfy the desire of a woman consumed by the fire of passion.

I had met Elisabetta at a party for the opening of Balbir's exhibition on the terrace of a Defence Colony flat. She was stunningly beautiful and occasionally reported for an Italian TV channel and also made documentaries on the issues affecting Indian women. I was more drawn to her personality. In any case, European women are quite bold. In the course of one of our chats she quite easily slipped in the nugget that in her teenage years she would masturbate any number of times.

At the party, in one corner a group was busy enjoying the puffs of hashish and a single cigarette was making the rounds. Elisabetta stood next to me and offered the cigarette to me too. Though a non-smoker, I couldn't refuse the Italian beauty's rousing invitation. It wasn't hashish but the sap of her lips which gave me the ticket to a beatific universe.

She lived in a Lajpat Nagar barsati. One day I landed up at her room in the afternoon when, in view of my being a non-smoker, she thrust a tiny piece of Afghan hashish into a pin and lit it. I was supposed to inhale the hashish from the other end of the pin. But I found hashish far less enjoyable whereas the act of pressing my nose against hers roused in me the magical feeling of a kiss. It was a divine afternoon.

Living in Delhi, Elisabetta had discovered the many ways of using pasta. She would boil *chhole* or *rajma* and mix it with pasta like an expert cook. I quite liked this fusion and would willingly help her out in the kitchen.

Once around this time Elisabetta, on her return from a trip to Kolkata, looked quite disturbed. She had fallen in love with an old Naxalite called Subodh. I would often land up at her place in the evening and listen to her interesting tales while enjoying red wine and *chhole*-pasta. I had told her that hashish was totally unsuited to my system. "You have your fill with it. As for me, simply watching you makes me feel relaxed." Who the hell wants hashish for that sort of comfort? The light of the red wine drew me towards her.

One day she began to cry as she talked about Subodh. I was astonished. Could a modern and independent western woman become so sentimental on falling in love? I saw her shedding tears... literally. Subodh had cleverly ensnared her in his web. I had seen his photographs. Also a video interview. He appeared to be a past master in the use of pseudo-intellectual vocabulary and our Italian beauty felt a kind of romantic affinity with his rebellious and violent past. She was unable to forget him.

I was looking for an opportunity when Elisabetta should herself walk into my arms and feel free and unencumbered. But she looked upon me merely as a good friend. That was my tragedy.

One evening I got sick of a boring party at an art show and landed up in Lajpat Nagar. I had already downed three or four pegs. Elisabetta was at home. But that evening she was rather unwell. She said: "Jai, I think I have slight fever."

She looked beautiful even in the middle of her fever. We were both in our own different worlds at that point in time.

"You must forget that rascal, that ruffian Subodh. He absolutely doesn't deserve your divine love. Just forget him."

"How can I? I'm at my wit's end."

"Shall I tell you an easy way out?"

"Way out? Have you discovered an easy one? Have you brought a herb from some mountain?"

"Yes. You can say that. You'd forget everything."

"Okay, I'd agree with you for a moment. Now tell me what remedy have you got."

"You might begin to laugh when I tell you."

"Why? What kind of a remedy have you got? Tell me! Now don't play games."

"If I offer you the divine pleasure of cunnilingus right now, you'd forget Subodh. I have a special expertise for this. Just as my brush attacks the canvas ever so softly, my tongue creates a somewhat similar magic. Do try it. You won't be disappointed."

Elisabetta didn't say word. Just continued to look at me for a while. Then said: "Will try your remedy some other time. Right now my whole body is feverish."

"No. Now is the magic moment. Don't let this opportunity slip by. I am also under the spell of a different kind of fever."

She looked at me with a sense of consternation, without uttering a word. Then she took out a bottle of red wine from the cupboard, lit a cigarette and continued to watch me.

"Don't misunderstand me Elisabetta. I don't want to have sex with you."

"So is cunnilingus something different from sex for you?"

"Yes, it is entirely different. Didn't I tell you, this is also a kind of magical art like putting colours on the canvas with a brush. And for you it'd work like *sanjivani booti*."

Elisabetta was a student of Indian mythology. She knew about *sanjivani booti.*

The next few moments were absolutely divine and magical for me. Elisabetta quickly removed all her clothes. She wasted no time. Her body was indeed quite hot. For ten minutes I was romping in the ocean of cunnilingus. One fever was cancelling out the other fever.

All of a sudden, in the middle of her fever, she began to mumble: "Fuck me Jai…fuck me Jai."

"I was in a fix. I was not prepared to meet her demand. I had a strange kind of sensation between my thighs. I found myself incapable of intercourse. As I stepped out of Elisabetta's house that evening I felt totally ashamed of myself. I had felt ashamed in front of the Italian beauty too though she tried her best to console me. But I was unable to look her in the eye.

Mathur had given me the phone number of a woman called Khushi. I contacted her. "I badly need a call girl. Send one right away if you can. I'd pay double her charges."

Chapter 4

A LONG STORY ABOUT A SMALL THING

In my college days, Ramashankar Pathak was my hero. His picture hung in my studio-like room. He had found incredible fame though he was barely 35. I had even heard that at an auction house in America one of his paintings sold alongside those by Picasso and Jeff Koons.

The moment I came to know about his latest show I decided to gatecrash its preview party. It was a glamorous gathering and some glamour girls were manning the gate with a proper register. Each invitation card was being vetted carefully.

I took courage and approached their desk. When asked to show my invitation card I told them I worked at Ramashankar Pathak's studio and was his assistant.

One girl said: "Let him go." But the other decided to phone Pathak, who told her: "Okay, let him in."

The moment I entered I grabbed a glass of beer and betraying all the seriousness of an art critic began to contemplate the paintings. Soon a western-looking lady walked up to me and began to talk about the paintings. Then Pathak came over to say 'hello' to her and asked me: "What's your name?"

"Jai Kumar. I'm a painter and a big fan of yours."

"But at the reception you were claiming to be my assistant."

"Yes sir, because those people were not allowing me to enter."

Pathak then said: "Show me some of your paintings. I'm sure you have some images on your mobile."

I showed him about a dozen of my works and he liked them. "Would you like to be my assistant?"

"Of course, sir. It's a big deal for me."

"You'll get a salary of 20,000. And it'll be a 10-hour day. You have a good hand. I have a lot of work for you."

Pathak handed me his visiting card. I was not really keen on becoming an assistant but an opportunity to work at Pathak's studio looked attractive. I also figured this might lead to some contacts.

I worked there for just about three months. In this time, I not only made paintings sitting in Pathak's studio but also prepared lunch every day. I also met Mathur the art critic for the first time in Pathak's studio. Pathak introduced me: "He is a talented boy. He'd become a great artist. And he makes fantastic mutton."

I was busy preparing mutton in the kitchen. Mathur and Pathak were drinking foreign Scotch. For me there was a bottle of rum.

"Mathur Saheb, you have come at a good time. I had a phone call from a New York gallery a while ago. They asked me why I was selling my works at such low prices in India. The prices should be the same everywhere. A four-by-four work by me now fetches 15 lakh and the same price will be charged in India as well."

Pathak had told all this to Mathur almost in a whisper, but I managed to hear the exchange. "And listen, my assistant must not come to know about my new prices. otherwise he'd immediately demand a raise."

Mathur laughed like a devil. That was my last day at Pathak's studio. I even gave up on my 10 days' wages. That day I decided never ever to work as an artist's assistant.

Later I ran into Pathak at a party. He said: "I think your rates have gone up. But you could have at least come over to collect your ten days' wages."

"Thank you sir. You should give that to your new assistant. Then he'd also be able to afford Scotch."

"Yaar, I certainly miss your mutton. You really cook very well."

"Do come to my shack sometimes sir. I'd treat you to lovely mutton."

"I'd definitely come. But only when you have your own studio. I've heard these days you are chumming with that brainless painter

Vipin. I can't stand that cunt." Pathak had a great aversion for Vipin Asthana.

I too didn't like him, but he had offered me space to paint in his large studio and didn't charge any rent. Since he was a pure vegetarian there was no scope to cook or eat mutton in his studio. And he kept away from girls. "They douse the creative fire blazing inside me. Falling in love means losing your very valuable time."

"I think you are a homo."

"Did I try anything in that line with you?"

"Weren't you an active member of the *shakha* in your young days?"

"This is the weakness of fake intellectuals like you. The *shakha* taught me discipline. Don't you notice I work for 14 hours every day? I don't drink nor go for cheap kind of womanizing like you do. I only have one duty – to go on painting."

When he arrived in Delhi from Mathura he was a simple studio painter who managed to occasionally sell a painting or two. He had a bed in the Lalit Kala Akademi guest house and dreams of becoming a Husain overnight.

Then a Gujarati builder divined a Ram Kumar or a Raza in his art. In those days an exhibition of his works was on in the small gallery at Triveni Kala Sangam where he could sell nothing for nine days. He would sit there all day, cursing the art market and the Congress. His theory was that the art market would improve only after the Congress was removed from the centre.

But a miracle occurred on the final day of the exhibition. A Gujarati woman by the name of Premlata was in the Bengali Market to have some *golgappas*. Afterwards, in the middle of licking an icecream she arrived at the Triveni gallery where Vipin Asthana's works immediately won her heart. She hardly had any interest in art, but the Indian art boom of 2002 had left a deep impression on her husband Amit. He would often regret not having acquired some Husain, Ram Kumar or Tyeb Mehta in the 1990s. At the time a gallery owner in Delhi had offered him a fairly large-sized Tyeb Mehta for 60,000 rupees which was not to be had for even 60 lakh today. He had promised Premlata that one day he'd buy the entire work of some young artist and offload it after ten years at manifold prices.

Premlata suddenly recognized those possibilities in Vipin's works as some kind of a divine miracle and immediately phoned Amit: "This young artist has somefantastic works. Why are you wasting time in Connaught Place? The real stuff is here. I'm going to book all the paintings."

"No, no. Don't be in a hurry. I'd be there right away."

Amit also began to weave dreams of the future on seeing the works. He told Vipin: "It's the last day of your show. I'd take everything. Tell me how much hard cash do you want?"

Vipin looked at the couple incredulously. Were they cracking some kind of a joke?

"I'd pay 10 lakh. If you say 'yes' right now then I should be able to arrange cash immediately."

"10 lakh is not enough sir. Even college students are selling their paintings for 2 lakh each these days."

"That's the problem with artists like you. You've been running your shop for the last ten days. Did you sell even one work? Have you ever seen 10 lakh in your life?"

Vipin was afraid the couple might change its mind. He had indeed never set his eyes on a sum as large as 10 lakh. In the evening he had the paintings loaded onto a van sent by Amit and the notes were counted by his wife.

Amit and Premlata were equally happy. Premlata now insisted on a second round of *golgappas*. Amit brought out the quarter of vodka from his car and handed it to the *golgappa* stall-owner. "Mix it in the water. It's my wife's birthday today."

The stall-owner was aghast. "Arre, what are you thinking?" Amit asked as he thrust a 50-rupee note into his pocket.

Amit and Premlata were celebrating as if they had stumbled upon a diamond mine. Vodka was showing its effect on Premlata in no time.

"Come, let's go to a hotel Prem, let's make passionate love."

The din and hubbub raised by the crowds below sounded quite

musical as it streamed in through the open window of their third-floor hotel room in Paharganj. For the first time Amit and Premlata experienced the singular joy of a shower sex that evening.

Actually, Amit recalled this delectable episode about a year later while buying one of my paintings. By then he had already bought some 250 works by Vipin and stored them in a godown. For him there was little difference between a painting and a sack of cement.

No wonder Vipin's misconceptions about himself were growing. The demand for his art had gone up. He had a new house, a new car and a new driver who had been hired from Mathura. His major plan was to get printed a lavish and expensive book on his art.

"It'll be an international-quality book. Mathur would write the introduction. And I'd have it couriered to all the museums in the world. Modi is coming and the Indian art bazaar is set to attain new heights."

Vipin was quite serious about his plans. He got hold of an upmarket designer in town and also spoke to the most expensive printing press.

"The size of my book must be quite large. I want it to be larger than the one on Husain."

Kamalkishore Agrawal, owner of the printing press, tried to suppress his smile. After Vipin had left, he phoned Mathur: "Sir, your *chela* seems to have lost his head. Wonder what'll happen to the poor guy once Modi comes to power."

"He is not an artist for me anymore." Mathur was in his familiar mood.

"But in the Introduction you have declared him to be a great artist."

"He gave me one lakh in advance. And more is on the way. Agrawal Saheb all these artists have now become cash-cows and you know very well cash-cows come very handy."

After this, I was at Mathur's house one evening where I discovered a very young woman pressing his legs with all the sincerity and devotion she could muster. She held herself back a bit on noticing me; since the main door was open, I had walked in without having to press the bell.

"Don't worry Jyoti. He's my special boy. We have no secrets between us."

I learnt that Mathur had gone to Kanpur where he ran into this devotee. She was being tormented by her businessman husband and in the meantime the frightful bug of culture had bitten her. She therefore decided to offer comfort to Mathur for a few days. Of course, after formally informing her husband.

"You are quite lucky Mathur Saheb. Cash-cows are at your service and goddesses of wealth are pressing your legs."

"It's *Madanotsav* today Jai Kumar. You'd also get some Scotch."

Mathur often used a peculiar kind of vocabulary to convey his meaning – cash-cows, *Madanotsav*. The latter meant the Festival of Dalliance.

"I hail you for your sex romps. But I must leave. At the moment I'm busy with my own fucking romps in the middle of poverty."

Jyoti smiled and quickly laid out some ice, a glass, and soda, savouries and Scotch on the table. She also liked to drink and was busy chain-smoking.

Mathur didn't want to revel in his dalliance alone. He was in a mood to go public with his private revelries.

"Mathur Saheb, you need to have your house repaired. There are cobwebs in the ceiling and the pile of magazines on the cupboard is gathering dust. Why wouldn't the mice be drawn to this place..."

"Don't worry Jai Kumar. This girl is staying here for some days and will fix everything. She's got hooked to the glamour of the cultural world."

I was surprised that a lovely and lissome girl like Jyoti should be pressing Mathur's legs in front of me without an iota of unease. Maybe she saw some great 'culture baba' in Mathur.

I quickly downed a Patiala peg of Scotch and said: "Jyotiji, hope you aren't a jealous kind of devotee. This culture baba of ours has a long list of followers like you. He keeps a diary and dutifully maintains their list."

"I don't care for his devotees. All I want from him is to learn the art of living. My husband taught me virtually nothing. He just fucked me and gave me a child. And now even that child lives away from me."

I said to Mathur: "Babaji, would you allow me to spill the beans? You seem to be in a good mood today."

"Arre Jai Kumar. You know that my life is an open book. You may tell her whatever you want. Jyoti has arrived here after knowing everything."

Jyoti gave me a lecherous look. "Okay Jyotiji, if another devotee of his has intercourse with him in your presence, would you accept that?"

"Well, my husband, who is a number one *gunda*, would do precisely this in our bed right in front of my eyes. At least Mathur Saheb is a sophisticated and educated man. With him even a threesome will have cultural overtones."

Mathur squealed with delight. Then sat her in his lap and began to caress her hair. I now realized this new follower was his super devotee number one.

"So shall we have a threesome?" Mathur asked me teasingly.

I thought the best course now was to leave. The very thought of seeing Mathur naked with his potbelly disturbed me. He was quite proud of his 'beer belly' though and would even claim girls too fancied it.

"You must clean and spruce up his house Jyotiji," I told her before leaving.

It was a time when Modi's *Swachchha Bharat* was just round the corner. Vipin had this belief that it'll bring revolution in the world of art. The confusion the foreign banks were creating in the art world would be removed by the new government and *Achchhe Din* was on the horizon.

Vipin made a lot of money in a very short span but also splurged quite a bit. But his style of spending money wantonly was all his own. He had a highly expensive book printed on his art, sent it to all the museums across the world, and courier boys could be seen delivering copies even at the homes of prominent artists. Some of them did keep it on their drawing-room tables for a few days. But I threw it in the wastepaper basket the very next day albeit after tearing out the page where the artist had scribbled a few words of affection for me. I didn't want to appear heartless.

On the contrary, Abha Bhalla, the glamorous owner of Enigma Gallery, didn't have any inclination to tear out the page with the artist's hand-written dedication as she flung it into the dustbin. Vipin had also gifted her a small painting. She immediately offered it to Khurana, the owner of her neighbouring gallery, at a throwaway price and then, showing off the cash in hand, asked me: "What do you think? It should at least pay for a Victoria's Secret lingerie."

But Vipin claimed he would never accept defeat. While he couldn't post anything on my Facebook wall, he started to leave meaningless comments steeped in devotion for Modi on some of my highly-interesting posts. I did delete them on one or two occasions but ultimately I was compelled to block him.

Four years into the Modi era, I one day ran into him at a gallery's 'dry' reception. He wanted to treat me to a coffee.

"I need a glass of chilled beer to put up with you. You might like to drink coffee of course?" I told him without blinking.

He obviously wanted to open up in front of me and so took me to a bar.

"So now you must be happy. Your government has done a lot of good for art. The *notebandi* must have taken your rates to sky high."

"Yaar, why are you hitting me where it hurts. As a matter of fact, I had some other dreams. This government hardly understands anything about art."

"Art is a kind of calamity for this government," I said as I tried to look at Vipin through the beer glass. His face looked surreal.

"Yes, I was mistaken. I have heard from my confidential sources that our Finance Minister had said in some private conversation that he would make sure Husain's rates collapses. Now you tell me, Husain Is a great painter. Where would we end up if his rates collapsed? We'd have no quarter left."

"But your ideological buddies were threatening to chop Husain's fingers."

"They are mad. What do they know about art? I do like the saffron colour but ultimately I'm a true artist."

"Husain is ours," I rather dramatically raised the 'Sahmat' slogan in front of Vipin.

"Yes, Husain is ours," he said rather sheepishly. That day I felt a fleeting twinge of sympathy for Vipin. He didn't appear to have completely gone over to the *knickerwallahs* camp. The artist in him hadn't yet died. Perhaps.

But Vipin's disillusionment with Modi surprised me. The fall of the art market had certainly brought artists like me onto the street, but lack of planning was to blame for the ruin of artists like Vipin. They had suddenly left behind the struggling life of a bag-toting artist and found themselves moving about in a Honda City, had fat volumes published about themselves, critics-for-sale had declared them great painters, and on the strength of their appearances as a hero on Page 3 of leading dailies they had begun to believe they were actually some kind of stars.

Even I had lost all my dignity in this glamour. I guess I too had become helpless like Vipin. The only difference was that Vipin could barely enjoy the fruits of his obscene success whereas I was under the illusion that I had enjoyed, at least to some extent, the short trailer of success life had shown me.

On that day even coffee seemed to create an intoxicating effect on Vipin. The acolyte was in full mood to make a confession that day.

"*Notebandi* was a wrong move. Look at Modiji, enjoying his world tour for the last four years. Didn't you read in today's paper that the Prime Minister's foreign jaunts had cost 1484 crores?"

"I feel good when you say all this. But I don't have high expectations from the opposition as well. Only the common man is honest today and that too out of compulsion."

When I returned to my studio, I was unable to decide whether to make a painting or read a book or watch *Crown* on Netflix. Then I noticed a number of missed calls from Khushi and phoned her: "Yes, what is it?"

"Sir, I have a small thing to offer. I phoned you many times."

"Small thing?"

"Yes sir, don't you follow? A small thing. And brand new."

"Does she know how to suck a sugarcane?"

"She'll learn sir. Shall I send her?"

"Send her to my studio right now. There's a packet of notes lying ready on the table for her. And don't talk too much rubbish."

Small thing. I felt like laughing out loud. Shall I give Khushi a painting? The poor woman has asked me for one ever so often even though I've never seen her. But she knows I'm a well-known painter. I had got Khushi's number from Mathur, one of those who take it as their birthright to enjoy life at cash-cows' expense.

Chapter 5

HUNDRED PERCENT CASH

When Mahesh Verma phoned me in 2007, to ask me to appear in his popular art programme *Tomorrow's Artists,* I was quite surprised. It's claimed that he was *the* hero of the TV world in the 1980s. It was a time when Doordarshan held the sway everywhere. Mahesh was handsome, his voice had a kind of magical timbre about it, he could have easily made a name for himself even in the world of modelling. In fact, he had started out his career as a model but from a young age he had also taken to the bottle. He would always carry a hip flask in his pocket and had such a strong liking for the Old Monk rum that its makers could have hired him as their model. When expensive liquor began to flow at cocktail parties, he would quietly fish out his hip flask and could be seen taking swigs wearing a permanent smile.

"I've learnt the art of not drinking free liquor from Om Puri. I was in Bhopal once to cover a films awards function organised by the Madhya Pradesh government. After the function that night I sat talking to Shyam Benegal at Jahanuma Hotel when Om Puri joined us. The waiter asked him: 'Sir, what will you have to drink?' Om Puri said: 'I have a Peter Scot bottle lying in my room. Bring it here. I only drink my own liquor.' From that day on I also decided to keep my own Old Monk in my pocket. From that day, it was good bye to free drinks."

Mrs Kasliwal had given my phone number to Mahesh. Though Doordarshan no longer wielded the old-time clout, Mahesh still managed to cast his magical spell in the art world. He was middle-aged by now and liquor had nearly wiped away his handsome looks, but he remained true to his love for the arts. Up until the afternoon, while busy at work, he would yet exude a kind of infectious charm. But by late night he would transform into a king of compulsive drinkers inhabiting some other world and progressing to end up as a swine. By 2007 people were beginning to avoid him or steer clear of him. But even in those days, when he arrived for a programme's shooting he would always bring along a beautiful girl as part of his team. Indeed, many of those beauties happily put up with him till late at night for God knows what magical attraction of his personality.

Nevertheless, when Mahesh set out to do his assignment, he would totally immerse himself in it. He made a fantastic half-hour programme on me for which he interviewed not only me but my mother as well. He also captured in his camera my childhood photographs lying in an old album. One picture showed me sitting crumpled in front of my father on his bicycle.

He visited me at my studio for three days with all his paraphernalia. But when I tried to gift him a small painting, he said: "Arre bhai, I'd certainly buy it when I have enough savings. I somehow can't digest anything that comes free."

"You take the painting now and pay me whenever you can."

But Mahesh Verma wouldn't relent. He took out his flask, took two or three sips, then lit a cigarette.

In those days a lovely woman called Sunanda would accompany him. I learnt that she was married and her husband was an officer in the railways. She had no children and the culture-vulture bug had bitten her hard.

In my studio, a DVD on the sex romps of some Italian models was lying on top of the DVD player. When Mahesh Verma brought his camera closer to it, I told him sheepishly: "Sir, please don't focus on it. Actually, it's a porn film. A friend had brought it from Greece, but I haven't watched it yet."

"Well, I have heard that Souza the great too was quite fond of watching porn films. A Mumbai painter told me that in New York he had seen Souza often get all dressed up and go out somewhere. One day, out of curiosity, he decided to follow him and found him buying a ticket outside a porn theatre. Though God alone knows why he had to polish his shoes to watch those movies.

"But sir, don't show this shot on Doordarshan."

Mahesh Verma laughed: "Arre bhai, I have to also save my job." I noticed that Sunanda was laughing.

When my programme was broadcast, I was left with this feeling I was an artist of a bygone era. As if the programme was being shown after my unexpected death. I felt embarrassed as I watched it though it made my mother feel quite proud.

One evening, after dark, as I was walking along the ITO bridge towards Mandi House, a car came to a sudden halt near me. Mahesh Verma stepped out and began to furiously kiss me on the cheeks. I could see Sunanda sitting in the car. Then he said: "Come, let's go to some bar in Connaught Place."

I realised he was stone drunk. But the attractive prospect of sitting and drinking with Sunanda made me agree.

I noticed that Mahesh was a familiar face for the bartenders, and they welcomed him cheerfully. I and Sunanda decided to have beer while Mahesh ordered Old Monk. The hip flask was not permitted to be taken out in the bar. He kept himself busy drinking without a break.

Soon it was time to close the bar. A waiter came up to us and politely asked for our final order. But even after the final order Mahesh continued to insist he wanted more. All the bartenders now stood around us with folded hands, pleading with him: "Saheb, we are also supposed to go home."

But Mahesh wouldn't relent. Finally, Sunanda took out her purse and settled the bill when Mahesh Verma picked a fight with her: "Why should *you* pay? Mahesh Verma doesn't drink on someone else's account."

"I'll take it from you later. Why are you worried?"

Somehow the two of us managed to persuade Mahesh to get up. But before stepping out of the bar he took out his hip flask and poured the contents on the carpet. The waiters said nothing, just watched the honourable TV star.

Thereafter we somehow managed to drop Mahesh at his house. It was a Doordarshan taxi and I decided to first drop Sunanda at her place.

"Tell me one thing Maa'm, how have you managed to put up with him for so long? Fine, he is a star. But isn't he a headache?"

"First of all, don't call me Maa'm. Second , tell me when are you going to show me that porn film."

"Why don't you come to my studio tomorrow. I haven't seen it either. It'll be great fun to watch it together."

As I was bidding her 'Good Night' I asked Sunanda a little hesitatingly: "Doesn't your husband live with you?"

"What? Is that a question? This government flat belongs to him only."

"But you are out till late into the night. Doesn't he object?"

"Arre bhai, so what if he has an objection. He would often assault me, so I had to file a report at the police station. Now if next time he raises his hand he'd have to go there straight away."

Then she came closer. The driver was watching us, but Sunanda was a bit 'high' by now. She kissed me on the lips and said: "Mahesh was kissing you on the cheeks but the right spot is this. Saala homo."

Next afternoon I waited for Sunanda for a long while. I had her phone number but didn't think it was proper for me to phone her. Three days later she was at my studio unannounced.

"At least you could have phoned."

"I wanted to give you a surprise."

On that day another artist, Shubhra Bansal, was also sitting in my studio.

Sunanda sprung a surprise on Shubhra by asking her: "Shubhraji, both of us are going to watch a porn film. Any objection?"

"Sorry, I don't follow. Why would I object?"

"Then you might as well join us in this holy programme." And the three of us sat down to watch the film. Shubhra watched it a bit scared and as soon as it ended, said: "I am in a hurry right now. I'll phone and come later."

"Have something to eat or drink."

"No, I'm fasting today."

"Oh, so we spoilt your fast by showing you a dirty film. Sorry."

"Why, there's nothing to be sorry about. Whether it's a good film or a dirty one it doesn't spoil the fast. In fact, I quite enjoyed the film." Having said this, Shubhra left, in the process giving us a fleeting glimpse of her frustration.

As I entered the kitchen to fetch a bottle of beer from the fridge, Sunanda followed me. It was time to give a practical shape to whatever we had learnt while watching the film. Sunanda was indeed quite beautiful though some ten years older than me.

"Didn't Vermaji leave you?"

"You don't know his situation. It's I who has left him. But he is a good man. Knows a lot about art and literature."

I had this feeling I was travelling in an old-time two-berth first-class cabin of the Indian railways. It's night and the light of the winter full moon is covering everything and both of us are bathing under its streams. It was an amazing journey.

Some days later I got this call from Mahesh Verma. "There's a programme this evening. A senior artist from Bikaner is here. I want you to have a dialogue with him. He was a student of Nandalal Bose at Santiniketan. He is also a fine artist in his own right."

"Vermaji, you are calling the wrong man for this dialogue. I know virtually nothing about Santiniketan and would be hardly able to speak in front of him. Mathur is the right person for this."

"Arre bhai, I want the artists of the young generation to hold dialogues with senior artists. These critics have had their day conducting their boring dialogues. Be at the studio at six in the evening. If you want, I can send the car."

It was not Sunanda this time round. Sangita, a new girl, was assisting Mahesh.

Shyam Bihari was 85 but quite alert in his responses. Even at that age he projected a kind of impressive dignity.

While we had tea after the programme, he said: "Come down to Bikaner some time and see my personal art collection. You'd like it."

Mahesh chipped in: "I am told you are very good at reading hands. Would you please read mine?"

Soon there was a long queue of those keen to consult Shyam Bihari. I was the only one who didn't show any interest.

All of a sudden, Shyam Bihari decided to read my hand. He said: "Your hand shows the sun. Fame will chase to you on its own. You won't have to do anything."

Shyam Bihari's personality certainly had a magical attraction. I learnt that he regularly went for a 10 km walk every day. He was rather thin and spare in built but at 85 looked not a day more than 60.

"I've heard that you were among Nandalal Bose's favourite students?"

"I can't say whether I was his favourite or not but even today he remains my *kalaguru*. The problem is that the young generation today dismisses these giants before even trying to know anything about them."

"That's because the Bengal School is a matter of history today. We have nothing to learn from those artists anymore."

"That's the problem. This thinking is wrong. You should read what they wrote and understand the finer points of their art. Abanindranath says that an artist is like the silkworm, nibbling away at the root. What the thread is for the silkworm, his style is for the artist; it imprisons him. But a time comes when he has to break those shackles to come out. And when he soars fluttering his wings, he becomes a true artist. He gets a new vision."

"Wow, that's it," said Mahesh. "Guruji, I'd certainly come and stay with you in Bikaner some day. One needs to keep a diary to jot down this profound knowledge. Now tell me Guruji, Is it true that Gandhiji favoured the covering up of the so-called obscene statues at Konark and Khajuraho whereas Nandalal Bose opposed the move?"

"The drawings of those Konark statues by Nandalal Bose are amazing though giving the illusion of being bawdy. They are among the finest specimens of art. When the Congress was debating its resolution at its Puri session some puritan leaders put up a proposal to grant funds to cover the erotic statues outside the temple with plaster. And they very nearly convinced Gandhiji. Dinkar Kowshik has referred to this episode in his biography of Nandalal."

"Then did Nandalal try to explain matters to Gandhiji?" Not only Mahesh, even I was curious to know the outcome of this episode.

"The issue was discussed at length. When they sought Nandalal's opinion on this he gave a straightforward answer – that covering the statues with plaster would be an anti-religious act. The sexual emotions get cleansed in the creative fire of art. The sexual emotion in life is the first step towards the stairs leading to one's final redemption or *moksha*, the others being religion and wealth. These opinions of Nandalal about art were the last words for Gandhiji. The dispute ended there and then. Otherwise, those Konark statues would have been spirited away by some grossly corrupt people."

The discussion with Shyam Bihari was quite fruitful. Then in 2016, I was invited to Bikaner for an art camp and decided to go and meet Shyam Bihari as well. He was in his nineties by then, waiting for a painless death in the final phase of his life. He appeared to be quite delighted on seeing me. He was resting in his bed but got up.

We had a long discussion. He had married when he was past 45. His only son Apoorva was not all that old. He ran a hotel in Bikaner while his wife Nandini was a math's teacher at a school. They invited me for dinner at their hotel.

"Why don't you try to convince father? He hardly listens to us. He has a large collection of super-expensive paintings and insists that we sell these and set up an arts college where the bright among the deprived children be given free education. Now, who would do that? You have seen his condition. He is hardly able to sit up."

"His idea is good, and you people need to do something meaningful in this regard. After all, Nandalal Bose had given away many of his important works to him free. So you also have a duty. I'm sure you are making a lot of money in the hotel business. Your bed-ridden father would feel good if he realises his son is going to fulfil his dream."

Not a word was uttered by either of them for a long time. Perhaps they didn't expect a Gandhian viewpoint from a comparatively young artist. In any case I too had reacted more seriously than I should have.

"Father not only has the Bengal School collection, he also has works by some other major modern Indian artists. You'd be surprised he also has a remarkable 1968 painting by Tyeb Mehta in his collection. I'm sure you know a number of art dealers in Delhi. If you could help us there, we'd give you 5% of the sale proceeds. We don't want your help for nothing," Nandini said, while Apoorva remained quietly busy on his mobile, as if our conversation was of no consequence for him.

"I think it would be better if you don't do all this while Shyam Bihariji is alive. You must let him live with the illusion that one day both of you will fulfil his dream."

"Yes, Jai Kumar is right. We need to wait for some time," said Apoorva.

"The market has been falling continuously. Look how much change has come about in the last ten years. If only we had sold the Tyeb Mehta in 2007…" Nandini's comment was worth considering.

Then unexpectedly, Nandini took out 25,000 rupees in brand new notes from her purse and handed them to me: "This is your advance. You can adjust it in your commission later on. You see , times are changing. To silently agree to everything the seniors say is like going back in time." I badly needed the cash and couldn't say no.

The news of Shyam Bihari's death followed my return to Delhi. I sent a condolence message to Apoorva and Nandini and put up an emotional post on Facebook which elicited quite a few comments.

Some three weeks later Nandini phoned me. I am arriving in Delhi for some work and will bring along the Tyeb Mehta painting as well. Please talk to some dealer. I'll send its image on WhatsApp. Forward it only to the major dealers. You know very well that Tyeb Mehta's works of this period are virtually impossible to get hold of."

"Why don't you try and sell it in an auction. There you can hope to gain much more."

"But in that case the tax will be quite heavy. Moreover, we don't want the word to spread that even before a year had passed since father's death we had started to sell works from his collection. Please understand how the gossip spreads in small towns."

What could I say! I figured a Tyeb Mehta could be sold quite easily and hoped to make anything from five to ten lacs.

I knew a dealer by the name of Goyal. No sooner had I forwarded him the image that he was at my studio, not bothering to even phone me.

"Yaar, do you think it's an original painting. How did a Tyeb Mehta reach Bikaner? One needs to look at the provenance too."

"Shyam Bihariji was a doyen of Santiniketan. It's quite possible that in the sixties Tyeb Mehta gave him a large canvas in exchange for some Bengal School drawing. Nobody asked for an authentication certificate in those days. There was no market for art at the time anyway."

"I have a very big buyer. He lives in Golf Links. If he likes the work a big deal can be cut in one day and both of us should roll in money."

"But the party wants 100 per cent cash. They have made it very clear. Shyam Bihari's son will only provide a certificate."

"Are you stupid? Nobody's going to pay 100 per cent cash. You'll get 30 per cent by cheque and the rest in cash. After all the buyer of such an expensive painting would also look for a proof of how he'd acquired it."

After a long discussion Nandini agreed to the 75-25 formula. 75 per cent was to be the cash component. "And it'll be sold for 1.5 crore. If the deal is for anything less, then I didn't want to be contacted. I know that in an auction it'll go for many crores. Not less than five to seven crores at least."

Goyal showed the work to his mysterious client. I was planted in front of a beer bottle in a Khan Market bar. Subsequently I learnt that a number of experts had been called over in the name of restoration. The painting was scrutinised thoroughly.

Goyal came to me in the bar and looked gleeful. I was to get 5 lac in the deal and he was to get 10. I was convinced Goyal was taking another 10 from the buyer. The buyer organised cash from his liquor vend in Moradabad that very night. I phoned Nandini: "Please arrange for someone to count the cash tomorrow."

"That's not a problem. My man has a counting machine. You have to just organise the funds."

Till late into the night Goyal sat with me nibbling at chicken drumsticks and topping it up with liquor.

The following day neither Nandini nor Apoorva would take my calls. I was quite distressed for four days and even considered visiting Bikaner. Goyal was also on the edge as he could see a large sum slipping out of his hands.

After four days Nandini sent a brief message: "I wanted 100 per cent cash and Enigma Gallery managed to organise it for me. Thanks."

Chapter 6

'AS LONG AS THE WENCH IS SWINGING AND COOL'

Goyal now headed for the Enigma Gallery to fight it out. He had clearly suffered a huge loss and hadn't slept for many days.

"I cannot accept this KLPD. My buyer suspects I've sold the painting to someone else for a larger commission."

"KLPD!", I couldn't help laughing out loud.

"What's there to laugh about? *Khade ling par dhokha*!"

"Your expressions are becoming ever more colourful."

"I still believe Nandini is cheating us. Nobody's going to pay her 100 per cent cash."

"Goyal Saheb, I know people who are keen to get rid of a truckful of cash in one minute."

Goyal hummed and hawed for about two weeks. He would phone me every day: "Anything new? Any message from that mean bitch?"

Singh, another art dealer, told me that Goyal was going to get a hefty sum out of the deal. "He wasn't telling you about his real commission. Actually, he was to get 25 lac from a Golf Links party."

One night Goyal opened the floodgates of abuse on the phone.

"Be patient Goyal Saheb! The party has a lot of stuff hidden away in the basement. Maybe we'd have better luck next time."

"I'd never ever speak to that woman. She doesn't know the ethics of business. The art bazaar is also a mafia of sorts and the mafia never goes back on its word. Once the word is given it's final."

"I've also lost 5 lac and it's a big blow for me too in my current situation."

But after that I stopped taking Goyal's calls. One evening Nandini too phoned me, but I didn't take her call either. I was indeed quite upset – with her as well as with myself.

The year 2018 had started out on a very bad note. While my debts increased the prices of my paintings continued to fall. But I could do little else other than paint. Even sex had become something of a black magic for me. The girls who once pestered me would now not even take my calls. Khushi alone picked up my phone.

"Sir, I have found a very good girl just today."

"WhatsApp me her photo."

"Believe you me, she would make you absolutely happy. It's not for nothing that I call myself Khushi."

"No, first send me the photo. I cannot splurge like in the past. My bank balance is down to zero."

Those were my worst days. But I never forgot Oscar Wilde's sage words: 'Even when in the gutter, we can look at the stars'.

In any case what else was I doing in the last three years other than looking at the stars from a gutter.

Then in the middle of this phase of adversity I got a phone call: "Sir, my name is Minakshi. I am a Bharatnatyam dancer. But I also paint. I want to show you my paintings. I am a trained dancer of course and painting is my hobby."

"Why are you addressing me as Sir? Do you think I am an elderly painter? I am only 34. Don't put me on a pedestal by calling me Sir."

"You seem upset. I don't think you'd recall but two years ago, in a page-three party picture I stood next to you holding a glass of champagne."

I did remember that picture very well. Minakshi was quite beautiful, perhaps 23 or 24.

"Shall I send my car?" she asked.

My car had become old and looked rather broken-down. It was quite a job to start it. I had to take it to the mechanic virtually every other day and even Shankar the mechanic was by now sick of it. One day he advised me: "Saheb, you better cover it with a nice painting and give it to a museum."

"Your idea is quite good," I said sheepishly. But I also knew that even that ramshackle car might fetch me 30 to 40 thousand rupees whereas if I made a painting on it, the poor vehicle might remain unsold. A collector had once made an offer to me: "If you agree to make a painting on my old car, I can pay you an advance of 5 lac right now."

But today the same collector, instead of buying a painting, was desperate to offload a painting bought for 8 lac for a paltry 80,000.

Minakshi's long limo showed she was a woman of substance. And once I arrived at her palatial house in Greater Kailash I thought I had arrived at some cultural museum. Everything was old. I could see no new paintings. The servant placed a glass of fresh juice next to me and sitting there I began to survey the room to spy where a painting by me could be hung.

Minakshi arrived in a beautiful sari. Her personality seemed to encompass the universal cultural excellence.

"You are quite wealthy. The house is palatial. What does your husband do?"

"Well, actually people like you own the real wealth. You are so full of talent. I had quite liked a particular painting of yours. Even wanted to buy it. But my businessman husband does not like modern paintings."

So I was wasting my time hunting for space for a large painting of mine in this drawing-room.

Minakshi now showed me her work. She was a Sunday painter and her canvases showed attempts to paint a range of dance postures. Still, they were not all that bad.

"I was married at a very young age. Around the time I arrived in Delhi people like you were page 3 heroes. The day my photograph appeared with you I was in the seventh heaven."

"Your husband must have been highly annoyed on seeing the glass of champagne in your hand."

"Not really. He believed it was a glass of juice."

There was a brief silence. In my hardship phase it was beyond my ken to seduce this woman larded in culture.

"Would you please guide me on how to stay on page 3? Some dancers seem to be all over the media. They are turned into prima donnas overnight."

"They also make the editors happy. Will you be able to do all that?"

"You tell me how to go about it? At the end of it I'm a housewife. A dancer confined to a grand and beautiful palace of culture."

I was beginning to get bored. I came home and phoned Khushi: "Send me someone."

"I don't have your choice right now."

"Then send across some second-rate girl. In my situation even she would look like a fairy."

When the bell rang and I opened the door, I saw a girl who looked like a eunuch. But for some reason, at that moment she looked more beautiful than even Minakshi.

In the evening I left for the India International Centre. There was a lecture by the eminent and senior art critic Samir Bannerjee from Kolkata. I had a casual acquaintance with him. Once he had included one of my paintings in a show on the subject of 'Spirituality and Art'.

I had told him then: "My art doesn't even remotely have anything to do with spirituality. In this show my painting would look like an outsider."

"Absolutely right. That's what I want. I need only an outsider."

When Bannerjee met me after the lecture he seemed quite affable. "I am staying at the centre until tomorrow morning. But I want to be in Delhi for a few more days. Could I stay in your studio for some days?"

On his last visit he had stayed at Anandmay's and I had gathered from his conversation that the old man had tried to flirt with his wife.

"The Moscow Biennale curator is a friend of mine. I am advising him to create a separate section on spiritualism. He is a Japanese, so he might agree."

Such words sound like music in one's days of adversity. The following day I invited Bannerjee to stay in my studio for a few days; I thought let me observe this determined oldie and wondered how he managed to attract women even in his dilapidated condition.

The very first morning, as I entered my bathroom looking for something, Bannerjee sans his dentures came face to face with me.

"Arre yaar, you should at least knock on the door!"

I stepped back with a smile.

But Bannerjee must have been practising some kind of magic. My maid Divya [yes, nowadays some maids do flaunt such names] had been working in my house for a year. In any case I have this principle that one must keep away from housemaids. Never try to share bed with them because then it becomes well-nigh impossible to make them do the household chores.

I did have a spare key for my studio-home. One afternoon, as I arrived home, I heard some desperate noises from near the kitchen sink. When I looked in I found Bannerjee busy showing off all his feats while Divya leaned against the sink tap bearing the full force of his exploits. But she didn't look unhappy.

Afterwards, as he emerged the toilet, Bannerjee told me: "I'm going out for a walk. Couldn't go in the morning."

Divya stood there with her head bowed.

"Your husband is going to give you a thrashing."

"That he does any way." There was no tinge of uneasiness in Divya's response, rather it smacked of self-confidence. Rather, the way she said it sounded mischievous.

"Send in your mother-in-law from tomorrow. As long as this desperate grandfather is staying here you won't show me your face."

"What about after his departure?" Divya sounded even more mischievous.

"You may come then. Who would put up with your sick mother-in-law that long?"

What surprised me was that this old Bannerjee had brought a glow on Divya's face. She never even once claimed Bannerjee had tried to take liberties with her.

"Did he pay you?"

Divya fished out a 100-rupee note from under her blouse. Then said with a smile: "This is to buy a chocolate."

An imported chocolate was rotting in my fridge for months. I gave it to her and said: "Now get going. And don't you show me your face as long as that old man is here."

"Why do you call him an old man?"

"Because all his teeth are false," I was fretting.

"Don't you feel bad sir, but isn't *he* real? Even at my age I've lost five teeth. It's to do with the poor diet these days."

Bannerjee said nothing on his return from the walk. Just sat there reading the newspaper. I busied myself preparing *khichdi* in the kitchen.

"Are you upset or what?" Bannerjee opened up after a long silence.

"Why?" Why should I be upset? I would have been if you had raped someone."

"Was the girl happy?"

"Tell me something Banerjee Saheb, do you take Viagra?"

"That's a strange question coming from you. Your next question would be, do I dye my hair?"

"That you do in any case."

"But I haven't gone bald. Watch out, at my age you would be a bald man. And it's not a crime to make one presentable at any age. Nor is taking Viagra. The main thing is that the desire shouldn't die down. When Picasso was 90, he said in an interview that 'I can neither smoke nor have sex, but my desire has not died down.'"

"Mercifully, Viagra had not been invented in Picasso's time. Otherwise God knows how the rest of his life would have progressed."

Then the doorbell rang and I stood facing Minakshi. She hadn't phoned me.

"It's my birthday today. So please wish me," she chirped.

I wished her dryly, without any enthusiasm.

"I have a dance programme at Kamani Auditorium this Saturday and you have to come there as the chief guest. The cards are going for printing and I've come to obtain your assent."

"Minakshi, I am going very low these days. Trying to make the impossible attempt of counting stars from the gutter. I'd look like a cheap guest rather than the chief guest. Meet him – he is Banerjee Sir. He is one of India's renowned critics and art historians. Make *him* the chief guest."

Minakshi greeted Banerjee with a lot of deference. She nearly touched his feet but Banerjee held her hands.

"Arre Minakshi, what was this awful move? Banerjee Sir doesn't like all this. You should shake hands with her, embrace her. He is very young. Picasso is his role model."

"Jai Kumar, don't forget that your role model is Souza. And Souza counted Picasso as *his* role model."

As expected, Banerjee happily agreed to be the chief guest at the dance programme. Then Minakshi insisted that I be the guest of honour.

I now discovered that Minakshi was leaving for Vrindavan by car. Ever since her arrival in Delhi she had been visiting Vrindavan on her birthday.

"Any particular reason?"

"No, I just feel like. I feel good once I'm there."

"Your husband would also come with you?"

"No. Does he have time to spare? I'm going alone. Why don't both of you join me? We'd have a good time. The time will fly away chatting."

"No Minakshi, I'm not in a mood. Otherwise, who would decline the company of a beauty like you. Indeed, you are a beauty completely soaked in the syrup of culture. Take Bannerjee Sir along. He has a gift of the gab."

Bannerjee readily agreed. "I've never been to Vrindavan and it's been many years since I visited the Mathura museum. And now I have Minakshiji's company."

"Sir, please don't address me as ji. I also want to see the Mathura Museum."

Just as they were leaving I pulled Minakshi's leg: "Beware! Don't stop by at a guest house on the way. Bannerjee sir loses his heart quickly to any lovely girl."

"Won't you ever give up your mischievous ways? Which man doesn't like the company of girls?" Bannerjee twittered.

"But you are a Casanova. It would be wrong to call you a girl-fancier. And yes, do look after your dentures on the uneven road."

Maybe I was trying to warn Minakshi. But my each warning turned out to be a shining medal on Banerjee's chest. It's a strange world.

Bannerjee returned home late at night. He was certainly tired but his face glowed. I said nothing. Perhaps it wasn't advisable to poke him. Whether I was destined to go to Moscow Biennale or not, he was a powerful man. Why should I be unnecessarily nosey? I couldn't sleep till late into the night. Bannerjee's snores were grossly disturbing the peace of the wee hours. I thought he must have impressed Minakshi with his intellectual gab. Must have made numerous attempts to cuddle up to her. Many things can also happen in a running car at night. Bannerjee was sex crazy, not a sex addict like me.

Next morning, I found him crooning a Bangla song in full swing. The bugger must have done something slimy during the Vrindavan trip. After all he was a Krishna Kanhaiya.

But Bannerjee kept his lips sealed about Minakshi. Maybe he was keen on telling a lot but wanted me to ask the first question. But I also maintained a stony silence.

Bannerjee was quite serious at Minakshi's dance programme. Her husband was also there. Afterwards he invited all of us for a dinner at Hotel Oberoi. But whereas Minakshi was the queen of culture, her husband was not even remotely associated with it – he was 100 per cent agriculture. How could Minakshi put up with him?

Bannerjee was to leave for Kolkata on the Monday morning flight. It had been a painful experience letting him stay at my place. I was determined not to make the mistake again.

Divya's mother-in-law was unable to operate the washing machine, nor had I ever operated it. So, the mother-in-law handwashed all the clothes. In the process she stumbled on a condom in the pocket of Bannerjee's trousers and brought it to me, holding it like a dead rat.

"It's not mine. It's Saheb's."

But Bannerjee Saheb betrayed no embarrassment. He took it without uttering a word and put it in his bag.

Later, I told him: "Sir, you need to be careful. You didn't spare her daughter-in-law and now your peccadilloes are getting exposed in front of the mother-in-law."

"You have this habit of creating a dispute about nothing. These maids are used to seeing all this. And you were lying to me that her daughter-in-law was sick. I ran into Divya yesterday as I was on the way back from my walk. She was happy with me. Told me that Saheb had asked her to proceed on leave for some days. Am I a fool? Why do you feel so scared of me?"

There was no point arguing with him. The previous night I had taken him to an artist Narendra Pal's house where, even after downing five pegs he picked up a half-empty bottle of liquor. In fact, he put the bottle and the leftover salted nuts into his bag right in front of Narendra.

"Nothing should go waste," was how he justified it.

Next day Narendra pulled my leg no end on the phone. "Yaar, who was this Mahapandit you brought to my house?"

"Arre bhai, he is a big critic. And an amazing womaniser. The bugger wears dentures but remains on the lookout for 16-year-olds. Was telling me with lot of relish that once, while he was in the middle of cunnilingus with a Bengali girl, his dentures fell out and he somehow managed the situation with much difficulty."

Narendra couldn't help hitting the roof laughing. "Yaar, bring him over today as well. Let's hear his tales."

On the final day of his studio stay Bannerjee gave me the shock of my life. I could never have imagined it.

I would generally leave home to avoid Bannerjee's company. And would tell Divya's mother-in-law to leave early. He was good at cooking and would prepare the meal while I was away

Banerjee had promised me that on the last day he would prepare excellent fish for me. He had invited Minakshi as well.

Around 12 I left home to buy some cans of beer. Minakshi took only red wine and Bannerjee paid me separately to buy a bottle of a good brand.

Back home, when I opened the door I found Bannerjee lying on the floor right in front of me and a naked Minakshi on top of him in the throes of orgasm. I could never imagine that scene.

My sudden return seemed to matter little to both of them. As if it was all in the day's work. I put the bottle of red wine in the kitchen and busied myself with arranging the beer cans in the fridge.

The self-proclaimed housewife Minakshi picked up her clothes scattered on the floor and went into the bathroom. Bannerjee also put on his clothes and sunk into the sofa. He had taken out John Berger's *Permanent Red* from my bookshelf and was pretending to go through it quite seriously. It appeared as if nothing had happened.

Minakshi emerged from the bathroom all dressed up and looking smart and asked me "Do you need any help?"

We didn't talk much in the course of the lunch. Minakshi lavished a lot of praise on the fish Banerjee had prepared. Her face bore no sign of any embarrassment, anxiety or sense of inferiority. I continued to imagine her naked body all night. She was indeed quite beautiful. But what did she see or find in that dilapidated Banerjee?

Once Banerjee left for Kolkata I went over to Narendra Pal's studio, anxious to tell him the entire episode.

After two pegs Narendra came out with a perceptive remark: "Yaar Jai Kumar, we have a saying in our Magahi - *jab tak jawanka lot-pot, tab tak budhwa teen chot*!" ['As long as the wench is swinging and cool / The oldie can strike threefold with his tool']

Chapter 7

SECRET TALES OF A WIFE

After Bannerjee's departure, Minakshi phoned me on numerous occasions, even sent me messages, but I was in no mood to enter into any kind of dialogue with her. Maybe I was worried, afraid that even in front of her I might end up in the 'Elisabetta situation'. That she should say 'Fuck me' and I should find myself inadequate, helpless and drained of all energy. In fact, I found myself helpless even in front of the canvas. I wanted to paint, would pick up the brush but continue to sit, staring at the blank sheet.

One day Minakshi called me from another number. My caller ID was not working and I took the call.

"If you hadn't taken the call this time round I would have walked into your house."

I liked the way she addressed me.

"Were you being consumed by the fire of jealousy that you decided to ignore my calls and messages?"

"Whatever you suppose Minakshi. The truth can be seen from many angles. But I liked it that day, when I saw you stop behaving like a helpless housewife. You can now certainly become a prima donna. There's no stopping you."

"I knew you'd say that. Tell me, when should I come to your studio. I want to see you right now."

"No, not in the studio. Meet me in the mall. We'd chat over a Starbucks coffee."

"Are you afraid I might shed my clothes in front of you? You have seen me naked and the principle of equality demands that I should also see you in the nude."

"Arre bhai, I'm not Michelangelo's David the sight of which would stir your bosom."

"Well, I'm not a Venus either."

"No, you *are* Venus indeed. You have a lovely body, as if chiselled by a sculptor. But what the hell were you doing with that old man? It was disgusting!"

"That's precisely what you cannot understand. The one you are calling an oldie with dentures is far superior and artistic than any number of handsome men. In fact, compared to him, my husband is a pygmy and a useless man. And I'm beginning to have doubts about you as well."

We met at the Starbucks and chatted for two hours. Finally, almost accepting defeat, I told her: "You are so heavily soaked in the cultural perfume that perhaps I cannot satisfy you. I feel I should not appear inadequate in front of you. It's a paradox that there was a time when I would be mad to possess women like you and today here, I am spurning you."

"Why are you turning yourself into a psychopathic case study? Can a call girl alone give you *khushi* now?"

I was taken by surprise. "Call girl... Khushi...Who told you all this? Bannerjee?"

"Nobody has told me anything. I'm just making a statement."

I didn't have the courage to take Minakshi to my studio. For a moment, I thought I should take a Viagra. But finally I took a quiet and formal leave of her.

Dr Anil Gupta had once bought a couple of my paintings. I decided to consult him.

"Look Jai, it's better if you avoid Viagra at 34. You have a different problem. The decline of the art market has created many complications and frustrations within you. If you can have sex with a call girl then you can very well have it with your girlfriend. You need to break the iceberg within. What you can see, within that exists an even larger part which is not evident to you."

After talking to Dr Gupta I phoned Khushi again.

"Do you have anyone?"

"Yes, that Bhutanese."

"The one with colossal breasts?"

"Yes, yes, that's the one."

"Send her."

"Okay."

"Now tell me, we have been talking to each other on the phone for so many days. Why don't you come over to my house one day? Come along with the Bhutanese today. I want to see you."

"Khushi is not something to be seen. It's something to be felt."

"Your WhatsApp account has a giggling baby's photo. I am very keen to see you."

"Have patience. Perhaps you'll see me one day."

The following evening, just as I was leaving the Central Secretariat metro station, I heard a familiar voice behind me: "Arre, Jai…"

When I turned around, it was Dharmvir Sinha. If he hadn't called me by my name, perhaps I wouldn't have recognised him. His face had puckered badly. He was a heavy drinker anyway, but his 50-year-old face bore the wrinkles of an 80-year-old. On his one shoulder hung his familiar bag with his laptop and some other tools. His shoulders looked quite lean now and carrying such a heavy bag was not all that easy for him. Will I also look like him after a few years? The very thought scared me.

Dharmvir had been the art director of a magazine for a long time but had quit the job some ten years ago. Now he went around with his laptop looking for freelance work. Though I had met him after a long time I heard about him often. The Press Club bar was his permanent haunt, but I never fancied its ambience since it reminded me of an opium den.

"I've heard you're quite wealthy now and your paintings sell for many lakhs," he said as he patted me on the back.

"If only you had met me some years ago, when I could perhaps claim I was selling my works for lakhs. But now I'm penniless just like you. Maybe worse than you. This art world is a big cheat."

"Fine. Now tell me something. I had gone to a cocktail party with you once where we met Syed Haidar Raza."

"Yes, I remember it very well. But Raza Saheb is no longer with us."

"Actually, at the time I was carrying a sketch-book which I handed over to Raza Saheb. He was in a wheel-chair and put down in my sketch-book his autographs in Hindi and English with a lot of warmth. His handwriting was quite calligraphic."

"Didn't he make a sketch or something?"

"No, only put down his signatures. But quite large signatures. They very much look like his sketches. One of Raza Saheb's followers had told me then that they might sell for a lakh."

"Had it been a sketch I could have got you something for it. But the signatures alone have no value – at least not in the current art market. I have the autographs of the Nobel winner writer Gunter Grass but nobody wants to buy them. I might be able to sell them in Germany on the Net though."

"Arre yaar, think about it. It's the signature of the great artist Raza. They look like he has made a sketch. His handwriting in Devnagari was amazing."

"You are right. But today you'd be lucky if a collector or a gallery owner were to give you even two or three thousand rupees for it. Yes, if you had tried to sell them around the time he put them down you might have got something."

"But do keep an eye open for a buyer yaar. You have good contacts. You'd also earn some commission."

"Yaar, why would I charge you a commission? You are a friend."

He gave me a hug and asked me in a low voice: "Tell me one thing. Did you actually sleep with Madhavi Sinha? I used to trust you a lot. But people say even *you* had an affair with her."

"It's better for you to forget Madhavi. At least I have. One day I did meet her at a cocktail party, but her second husband dragged her away. I think it was better that way."

Dharmvir now clung to me and sobbed openly: "Yaar, I am ruined. Watch out, one day I'd be found dead on the road and people will take away my laptop while I lie there like a dead dog. And if I don't die like that then I'd put a rope around my neck and hang myself from the fan. There's no work to be had anywhere"

I remained quite disturbed all night, thinking about Dharmvir's miserable situation. How people dream of selling the mere signatures of

Husain, Souza or Raza for millions. Hollywood star Anthony Hopkins (who has played Picasso on the screen) once said that 'I no longer give my autographs to fans since they put them up for sale on the Internet right away'. One of my cousins worked for Air-India. Once Husain was sitting on his desk to have a ticket issued. My cousin asked him to draw a horse and he obliged and even signed it. Husain and Souza were quite liberal in a way. Today's eminent young masters refuse to give even an autograph. Anyway, my cousin wanted to sell the sketch for some 15 or 20 lakhs. He had studied all the auction catalogues and kept a proper record in a diary. One day, in a fit of pique, I told him: "Yaar, you better keep your Husain. Why do you want to sell it?"

I now recalled many emotional moments involving Dharmvir. When I was around 23 and he was close to 40, both of us got a lucrative assignment in Mumbai. But while he had to stay there for a fortnight, I had to return home after only three days. We had gone by Rajdhani Express but I was to return by air.

As soon as it was 7 in the evening, there was an announcement in Rajdhani that hard drinks were not allowed in the train. And lo! The waiters were on the ball immediately. Those thirsting for drink would start to make their pegs. And each one of them wanted to get sozzled before the hot tomato soup arrived.

Dharmvir downed four pegs in no time. Then he came over to me and whispered in my ears: "Before leaving I had made full arrangements about my wife."

"You mean the rations for a fortnight?"

"No yaar, you are still a kid. You must understand. There is a secret posture, *Dhanush Asan*. That's it. Just before I left I put her on that *Asan*. Now she will have no desire for a fortnight."

"Desire? Desire for what?"

"You are stupid. Desire for sex. I had learnt this *Asan* with great difficulty. It just locks everything up."

"You mean it works as some kind of a chastity belt?"

"Yes, you can say that. I can teach it you too. But you have to first get married."

"Sinha Sir, I think there is also a kind of risk in this *Asan*."

"Where is the risk? When I first put her on this *Asan*, Madhavi told me she didn't have any desire for a month. She even began to hate the word Sex."

"But I believe this kind of *Asan* might also dramatically rouse a woman's sexual desire."

"You better keep your opinions to yourself. You are talking nonsense. This is a tried and tested recipe."

Dharmvir poured a peg even into his tomato soup. He was living in his own world whereas I was busy spinning my own fantasy. Madhavi Bhabhi appeared to me as one of Hemen Mazumdar's sexy beauties in a wet sari.

One afternoon Dharmvir bought, after a lot of haggling, some foreign soaps, perfumes etc. from Mumbai's Fort area. Then he made a packet and told me: "Deliver them to your Bhabhi as soon as you reach Delhi. That should cheer her up."

As long as I was with him in the hotel room Dharmvir was a gentleman. But the day I was to catch the flight he organised a nude model. I kept wondering that if Dharmvir were to put the call girl on his special *Dhanush Asan* the poor woman's business would go bust. "Don't put her on a wrong *Asan*," I whispered to Dharmvir as I took leave of him.

We really slogged hard for three days in Mumbai. I had to make a 15-foot long and 7-foot high painting in the hotel lobby. I worked quite vigorously in those days. The hotel owners wanted a colourful abstract. In a way I was to daub colours on the wall. Dharmvir had taken on quite a few assignments to decorate the newly-built hotel. But I was to finish my work in three days and leave.

Every day, by the evening we would be so dead tired that we'd reach our room and settle down with a bottle of liquor and order the room service to send in the dinner. Most of Dharmvir's chatter was limited to his girls and sexploits. If an opportunity offered I would chip in with some juicy stories as well.

On the very first night Dharmvir warmed up and began to retail stories with quite succulent and intimate details about his wife. We didn't have many issues to talk about any way. Men do normally tell stories about their girlfriends, colleagues or even neighbours but remain quiet about any intimate details about their wives.

When Dharmvir opened up with his highly personal stories laced with titillating details they inspired within me a pleasure of a different sort. I would listen to him in complete silence, making almost no comments. But his tales would work as balm for my fatigue. Then I'd dream only of Bhabhi.

I had visited Dharmvir's house in Delhi only once. It was a tiny flat in Patparganj. He had no children even after seven years of marriage. Madhavi was a very sociable person and quite fetching too. She said: "Dharmvir told me you make very good portraits. Why don't you make one of me."

In those days I always carried a sketchbook, colours, brush and other art material in my bag. I made a seductively beautiful portrait for her. She was very pleased and told Dharmvir: "Let's go and have Gujarati thali for dinner. I am sick of cooking the same old fare every day."

The restaurant was close by. Some two km away. Dharmvir took out his scooter and told me: "You are so thin and lean you might also sit in the back. But don't try to cling to your Bhabhi too closely otherwise she'd be annoyed."

The scooter stalled half way through. Dharmvir began to desperately kickstart it but it won't.

"Earlier you'd start it with one kick. Now you are busy kicking it with no result."

The remark left me squealing with laughter. And then all of a sudden the scooter started. This time round I took full advantage of the closeness of Madhavi's shapely hips. I didn't care for her annoyance. And why would she be annoyed anyway?

On the way back I had to collect a packet of all the forbidden foreign magazines (*Playboy, Men Only*) from Dharmvir. He had told me that a painter needed to have those magazines to study nudes. He had a big packet ready for me. I waited at the door with Madhavi. When Dharmvir handed me the packet, she said mischievously: "Why are you spoiling the kid?"

"The kid is already spoilt," Dharmvir said.

Now, all the many delightful stories Dharmvir had related in Mumbai got linked with this brief meeting and no sooner had I landed in Delhi that I headed for Patparganj with Madhavi's packet. I didn't even bother to phone.

My arrival with the packet cheered Madhavi. She said: "You should have lunch here. I'm preparing *rajma*-rice."

"That I'd have begged for it anyway, even if you hadn't invited me."

"Okay, now tell me do you have a girlfriend?"

"I don't make friends with just one girl. I have many."

"You're quite smart."

Madhavi was certainly charming. But having heard all those intimate stories about her I was looking at her in a different way. When you look at a woman like that, she senses it immediately.

"Why are you looking at me like this?"

"No, no, there's no reason."

"There *is* something. You are avoiding eye contact. I know you are not a kid. Why were you pinching me on the scooter that day? What if I had told Dharmvir?"

"What could have happened? He would have scolded me. That's all."

"And I would also have given you a thrashing."

"I would have loved that."

I had a big weapon to lay Madhavi there and then – the many private and intimate details about her life. But I started out with *Dhanush Asan*. "Bhabhi, tell me for a fact, does *Dhanush Asan* actually suppress all desires for days and days?"

"So you have been told even about that? My husband is really an idiot."

"I am dying to know for sure. I don't agree that any *asan* of this kind can suppress the desire for sex for some days. For all you know it might even increase it."

"You are right. But every time he leaves on a long trip he goes away with the misguided belief that his wife won't be troubled by any carnal desire. What actually happens is just the opposite."

The moment the discussion took this turn the sense of unease between me and Madhavi disappeared entirely. She was perhaps 12 or 13 years senior to me. People say that around the age of 35 a woman's sexual desire is at its peak.

As I slowly retailed to her the most intimate and succulent details of her life, initially she was shocked. She even abused her husband. Then gradually she began to enjoy the situation on realising this man was already privy to all the unmentionable details of her life. He even knows that the left side of the most secret part of my body has a large mole.

"Bhabhi, please don't tell him that I have shared everything with you."

"I won't tell but I have a condition."

"What?"

"You would draw me in the nude. Now, right away."

"But you won't be able to hang it in the house." My earlier portrait, nicely framed, hung in the drawing-room.

"Which idiot says you'd make it for me? I'd only be your model. You hide it away in one of your albums. When I become old, I'd come over to your place to see how I looked in my youth."

I started to take out from my bag the material to make the portrait before Madhavi could change her mind.

Madhavi went out through the back door and put a lock on the main gate. She was afraid her friends in the neighbourhood might drop by unannounced.

Just as she was preparing to take off her clothes there was this phone call from Dharmvir in Mumbai.

"Darling, have you got my gift packet? Jai had told me he'd deliver it today."

"Yes, I've got it. He delivered it just now. I had insisted he should have lunch here but he didn't stay. Was in a hurry. And I'm now going to take bath with the soap you have sent. I have just taken off all my clothes."

"You've made my day by saying this darling!" Madhavi had put the phone on the speaker.

Fearing he might make some vulgar comment Madhavi then cut the phone and took off her clothes in a jiffy. Her naked figure would surely have been any artist's dream.

But instead of making her portrait I considered it more urgent to slake her carnal passion roused by the effects of *Dhanush Asan*. Perhaps it was the effect of that *Asan* that every time one tried to douse the fire of desire in Madhavi it would flare up. The consequence was that while Dharmvir was away in Mumbai I had to make quite a few trips to Patparganj.

Do I have to say that those days were among the best in my life? One day I also drew a nude of Madhavi and she captured it on her mobile phone.

"What if your husband finds it?"

"Arre, does he have time to see my album? In any case my mobile is always locked so there's no such danger."

I still have that portrait in my collection. A collector is very keen to buy it. He is after me. But I've told him: "Not for sale."

After two years Madhavi eloped with the owner of a mobile phone shop in the neighbourhood market. He would change his mobile every two months. Then one day he realised it was time to change her husband.

I had lied to Dharmvir when I said I had run into Madhavi at a party. Actually she had phoned me some three or four years after her second marriage (Dharmvir had divorced her immediately, accepting in the court that he was impotent).

"How are you?"

"I'm all right. But all husbands are alike."

"What do you mean?"

"All of them are looking for ways to devise the *Dhanush Asan*."

"Do you have any children?"

"No. I guess I am barren."

I called Madhavi over to my studio and on that day didn't use the condom on purpose.

Since that day I have been looking for Madhavi. I have this feeling I have my child somewhere. Today I ran into Dharmvir, may be another day I'd find Madhavi too, with a lovely little girl (no, I don't want a boy! They are so naughty!).

Chapter 8

AND THEN THE BANKNOTES RAINED!

I believe my mental and physical decline began on 8 November 2016. I had already received a jolt in 2008. But the *notebandi* by the government had the worst effect on the art world. It's not as if the *notebandi* has managed to control or reduce the 'cash' market of art. Indeed by 2018 people have nearly forgotten the moment when it was assumed that henceforth everything would be settled through cheques, all funds would go into banks and there'd be no escape from the income tax. On the contrary what I notice is that art galleries are freely dealing in loads of cash. On top of that the 2000-rupee notes have further reduced the 'burden'.

Old-timers recall the days when a notorious gallery owner would carry sacksful of 10-rupee bundles in his car. Once a deal was finalised with an artist he would promptly phone the driver: "Okay, now bring in the 10-rupee sacks."

Which artist would have the strength to count those 10-rupee bundles? Hail the 2000-rupee note!

Amit Prakash is among the country's senior artists and is often to be seen all over Page 3. He gets fidgety if he doesn't receive a party invitation. I met him at a party once and he looked quite worried.

"Yaar Jai Kumar, you know the pulse of the entire art world. Immediately after the *noteband,i* Enigma Gallery had called me up to say 'We had only four paintings of yours and all of them have sold. We are sending your full payment through our driver.' But when the driver arrived, I was surprised to find that 3 lakhs were in old notes. I was furious and returned the entire payment."

"You made a mistake there. You should have kept that cash. At that time there were at least some ways to spend those notes. You won't get your payment easily now."

"That's the trouble. When I phone them, no one picks up and when I send a message no one replies."

"Imagine, when a senior artist like you is facing this situation what would a young artist do."

Initially the young artists whose works sold few and far between were happy with the *notebandi*. They had this misguided notion that the rattled collectors and galleries would now spend the old notes on their works. But the offers some of the brilliant young artists did eventually get were not all that hefty. The galleries were still keen on buying works against modest amounts of cash. Actually, even the old notes were looking for masters such as Souza and Raza.

An art street had come up in the Lado Sarai area in Delhi where galleries of all shapes and sizes had cropped up like mushrooms. Then suddenly started to shut down. Why? The builders' wives flitting about like flies in the glamorous art world also disappeared suddenly. Why?

On the other side, the media had so hyped the glamour of the art market that middle-class parents suddenly began to push their children to go for arts studies. And once the private universities in the country tasted prosperity, they also introduced upmarket art courses.

Recently, I was to make a painting in front of a group of students from one such university. There, the VC's all inquiries were focused on the subject of whether or not the arts students were likely to get job offers on the campus.

I told him: "No chance. Only some of them might land some minor posts as art teachers. The rest will have to do freelancing." The decline of the art market had made even freelancing nearly impossible. Manjit Bawa would say that while magnifying the exceptional success stories of three or four artists the media forgot that 95% of the artists were either unsuccessful or struggling. An ordinary Patna college did not give rise to a miracle like Subodh Gupta based on any logic or some historical destiny. While the Patna teachers might pat their own backs today, they were not in the mould of K G Subramanyan who could create a favourable atmosphere at Santiniketan or Vadodara University.

The VC looked at me as if I were a curiosity.

The parents of the art students who were being asked to pay large sums as fees were bound to ask what kind of lucrative job their wards were likely to land. Thus, both the students and the teachers in these institutions with state-of-the-art facilities were essentially 'outsiders'. The institutions didn't look upon Van Gogh or Picasso as role models. Their biographies did not inspire the students. There, Van Gogh would be declared a mad man who cut his ear at the prodding of a prostitute and Picasso would be looked upon as a middle-aged lecher who, at 45, had made a 17-year-old model his wife. The 'Me Too' movement is tearing into smithereens Picasso's life and his relationships with women. The largest number of names in the list of the 'Me Too' movement are those of eminent cultural icons.

When I reflect on all this, I sometimes find myself in the illusory world of a psychedelic universe. For a moment I feel I am confined to a mental asylum. Both my passion and worries are real. But the strange conditions prevailing in the art market are making me impotent in every way.

"You need to quit the world of art for some days," was the sage advice of my JNU-style intellectual friend Sonali.

"What else could I do?"

"Whatever. But leave the world of art otherwise it'll send you to an asylum one day."

"Why leave for some days? Why not forever?"

"Look, there should always be the option of coming back. May be you'd be able to revive your intellectual cells then."

"I believe that one should quit the art world for ever without remorse. If one means to come back, then why leave it in the first place? Why not continue to live there and eventually die there? History has seen many artists who either swiftly met their end because of their insanity or other people's insanity finished them."

Sonali looked at me in silence. She was my first intellectual friend. I could lie down naked next to her and yet we could talk about everything under the sun except sex.

She would change clothes in front of me without being uneasy.

Once, as we were in the middle of a discussion – we were talking about Schopenhauer's view of revenge being sweet sometimes - I said to Sonali: "I want to touch your breasts for a second."

"Go ahead."

I touched her by pushing my hand under her top.

"Did you feel anything?" I asked.

"Nothing."

"Then why do the unnecessary hard work? I have had sex at every conceivable place. Vehicle, bullock-cart, motorcycle, palm tree, Rani Rupmati's ruins in Mandu, the open skies of Khajjiar, airplane toilet…"

"And what did you achieve?"

"That's precisely what I fail to figure out. I once fell so madly in love with a girl that I had my life's possibly the most glorious intercourse with her. Later that night I had to leave for Chandigarh. It was winter time. Just as I landed in Chandigarh the following morning, I spoke to the girl on the phone and she invited me back. 'I'm leaving for Spain for six months', she said. That was it. I picked up a blanket and took the bus the very same night. I had a mountain of work to do in Chandigarh but put all that on hold and landed up in Delhi. My friend was to fly out in the afternoon. Had I returned for sex or was it true love?"

"You returned for sex. Only for sex. If it were true love you would have felt her presence even away from her."

"Maybe you are right. Maybe I was never truly in love. I considered only cunnilingus as true love. My friend had said, 'During cunnilingus you use your tongue like Picasso's brush'. The Picasso Museum in Barcelona has a small but stunning work by Picasso, created when he was a young man of 22 or 23. A youth is licking a girl's vagina. It's an amazing – almost spiritual - depiction of cunnilingus.

"Agreed that sex is important in life. But you seem to give it far more importance than it deserves. Yaar, there are other issues to mope about."

"Souza gave a lot of importance to sex. Picasso…"

"Yaar, they were geniuses. Can you draw a great line like Souza did? What is it that's yours, Jai Kumar? Don't live under the misguided belief you are as great as Souza. You are not even mini Souza!"

Sonali was speaking the bitter truth.

Mathur called me up the next morning: "Jai, if you need cash go to New Direction Gallery. I've heard its owner Mohit Gupta is buying up stuff worth crores. You'll get old notes but that shouldn't make a difference to you. You can easily deposit them in the bank."

"Do you remember Mohit had come to me once to ask for a painting? And I had ticked him off at the door itself. The uncouth cloth merchant was planning to open an art gallery and what had he named it? New Direction!"

"Times change, people change, and you also need to change Jai. Just forget what happened."

When Mohit Gupta arrived at my studio for the first time some ten year ago, I didn't know him. He was extremely polite and showed a lot of respect to even a young artist like me.

In those days there hung on my wall a limited-edition poster of Manjit Bawa in a frame. Before he went into coma Manjit was on a visit to a gallery where I had asked him to sign the poster. It already had his signatures in English. Below that he signed in Hindi with a pencil for my sake.

Mohit Gupta kept looking at the poster. Then asked: "Are these signatures genuine? I mean are they original?"

"Yes, absolutely."

"Then I want to buy it."

"My price is 20000 rupees."

Mohit immediately took out his wallet and handed me 20000. And left in the belief the poster was an original drawing. He even forgot he had come to me to buy one of my paintings.

An hour later I got a phone call from him. He was agitated: "It's a poster Jai Saheb."

"Who told you?"

"Mathurji."

"And when did I claim it was an original drawing? You asked me whether Manjit Bawa's signatures were genuine."

"But..."

"No buts and ifs. Your cash is still lying on the table. Return the poster and take away your cash."

Mohit came and without uttering a word put down the poster and left with the cash.

"It's better if you carry on with your cloth shop in Chandni Chowk. Else have some training before starting your art business."

After a few days he was again at my door, to buy one of my paintings. But I shooed him away from the door itself.

Down the years he rose to become a successful art dealer. He had his gallery in a basement which I had never visited.

Then one day I met Mohit at a party and was surprised by his warmth. And today Mathur was suggesting I should go to his gallery. Would it be all right? What if he humiliated me? But I was in dire need of cash and my debts were mounting.

After the *notebandi* I had assumed that collectors and gallery owners would now chase artists like us with bundles of notes in hand. But they were clever. They would like to acquire a Souza for 35 lakhs but won't touch a good young artist even for a lakh.

Even so, I went to Mohit's gallery and he greeted me quite warmly. He had a bundle of old 1000-rupee notes on his table and I eyed it hungrily.

"What brings you to this poor man's abode? You know already that we buy and sell paintings like bolts of cloth.

It was obvious Mohit was being sarcastic.

"I need some cash. I am suddenly facing some financial difficulties."

"You have come rather late in the day Jai Saheb. If only you had come a little early, I would have certainly helped you out. By the way I am buying up young artists' works virtually at the price of wastepaper. Perhaps you wouldn't have agreed to sell your works at that dismal rate. You know very well that everything is fair in love and business."

Evidently a piece of chicken had got stuck in Mohit's teeth and he was trying desperately to pick it out.

I was about to leave the gallery quietly when Ruchika arrived. I had seen her after many years.

"Good Ruchikaji that you have come! These bundles have been waiting for quite a while to have a feel of your delicate hands."

Ruchika quickly picked up the notes and put them in her purse without caring to count them.

"You better count them Ruchikaji. Sometimes we people also make a mistake."

Ruchika took out the notes from the purse and began to count them. Then for some reason stopped half way through and said: "Okay Guptaji. I am in a bit of a hurry."

Just as she got up to go I thought it was time for me too to take Mohit's leave.

"Jai Saheb, a friend of mine wants to get rid of some of his old notes. If a deal is struck I'd phone you and we could pick up 10 to 20 paintings from your studio as well."

I felt quite insulted. But who cared for one's dignity in the middle of depression in the art market. Actually, Gupta had welcomed me with a degree of respect whereas I had summarily shooed him away from the door itself.

Out in the street Ruchika was looking for a taxi on her mobile.

What is it? You seem to be in a tearing hurry. Let's go and have coffee somewhere. Though today being the day when you've earned so much, beer won't be a bad idea either."

Ruchika had been my class fellow in the arts college. We weren't very close though. Just limited to 'Ciao… Ciao'. But I knew that she had married and had a young son.

She agreed to come to a beer bar. There was a fairly big one in the mall close by.

"Mohit Gupta has struck a goldmine. He must have cornered the paintings for a song. But the artists are helpless today."

"Quite true Jai. He has bought my paintings really for a song. Don't get deluded by the bundles of notes. A hundred paintings were loaded onto a truck from my house. My husband was mightily pleased so much garbage was leaving the house. And my mom-in-law must have distributed sweets."

"Tell me one thing Ruchika. Didn't you choose your husband on the Internet? Then how come you have reached this point in such a short time?"

"He married me thinking that since I was a painter my works would sell for lakhs. People develop this misconception about art on seeing spicy stories about art auctions in the papers and on TV. In my case, the art market collapsed immediately after my marriage. My gallery had talked about paying me a monthly retainer but changed its mind and returned all my works."

"But your husband has a good job and surely draws no less than 1.25 lakh as salary."

"Yes, he has a good job. But the investment bug is eating into the motherfucker's brain all day. And I remain confined to the house. Can't smoke, and as for a drink I guess even the next seven generations of his family are not going to have one. He doesn't allow any pocket money either. And I have to buy my own art material. Even to watch a movie I have to dip into my own purse. All that he wants is a fuck every fortnight. Since I'm in a foul mood most of time, if I don't cooperate he goes into the bathroom and starts 'shaking'. I feel tied down because of my child. You cannot imagine how mean he can be? Says that while he'd pay the son's school fee, I should pay the tuition fee. At least the cash I've got today will offer me relief from hardship for a time. Otherwise I have to look up to him for every need."

"Go for a divorce. Why are you dying in such suffocating marriage?"

"I did try. But can I pay even the rent of a decent flat in Delhi on the strength of my freelancing? Impossible. Right now I'm only considering going off to Manali alone for a week. Should hire a cottage and just paint, smoke without fear and have Vodka. I am sick of this dog's life."

I was looking at Ruchika.

"I think you should have married a painter. He alone could have put up with your lifestyle. And even if he didn't drink himself at least he won't have objected to you drinking."

"Would you have married me?" Ruchika smirked.

"Perhaps I would have proved to be even more difficult than your husband."

"Then? You are refuting your own argument. All men are bloody bastards and one should keep away from them."

Ruchika now ordered another large Munich-sized glass of beer. She had the bundle today. So what if the notes were old. They could still be deposited in the bank.

"And what about that Rohit Bansal who wanted to buy your paintings?"

Ruchika had choice expletives ready for him as well. "Bansal was hardly a buyer. He was a bloody thief. He pressed me to take a small flat and offered to pay the rent in return for one painting every month. Actually, he wanted to have me as a keep. His wife had begun to look like his mother."

Everything that Ruchika said was the bitter truth. The framer Grover also had a role in spoiling her market. He would frame all her works for an exhibition but wouldn't charge her, instead retaining with him a number of her paintings. Ruchika too seemed to favour this arrangement.

But when the market collapsed, Grover sold to a big art collector 120 paintings for a million rupees. Of those 120 works, 27 belonged to Ruchika. Thereafter the gallery cancelled the arrangement and returned her remaining works. Grover had reduced the price of her works form one lakh to 10,000 rupees each.

"But I'm happy today. See how much cash I have!"

The beer had hit Ruchika hard. She took out 1000-rupee notes from her purse and began to drop them on the table. As a child I would sometimes accompany my mother to *kirtans*. And always noticed a woman, floating in the ocean of devotion, bawling: 'And then the banknotes rained!' In the bar I was recalling that woman: 'And then the notes rained!'

"Madam these are old notes. Do you mean to settle the bill with these?"

I tried to convince the waiter that those notes were for the bank and the bill would be settled with new notes or a credit card.

"You surely have new notes as well."

"Aren't these new? Do you think they are fake?" Ruchika had drunk so much she seemed to have gone out of her mind.

I had to now use my credit card even as Ruchika tried to press her old notes on me.

Then I thought for a moment and accepted five 1000-rupee notes from her. I recalled that the girls sent in by Khushi gladly accepted the old notes.

The bill for the beer came to 6500 rupees. I don't know whether Ruchika was able to reach home in one piece.

Chapter 9

AN EXUBERANT OLDIE

Ratanlal Parashar was an art dealer but a shady one, having been caught once in a case involving a fake Anjolie Ela Menon though eventually he managed to escape. One evening he decided to convert the table in his gallery into a bar and asked me give him company. Then he started on his sob story. "I have never ever done anything wrong," he whimpered.

"But you told me once that you had a 40-year-old maid and you not only exploited her but didn't spare her daughter either. Isn't that something unethical?"

Ratanlal stood up. Then, in the middle of trying to tighten his belt, said: "You are making fun of me. I respect you highly and am crying in front of you and you talk such rubbish. And an idiot like me offers you scotch and even orders a pizza for you."

Then his sob story resumed: "I always avoid any deals involving fake works. You know very well that I'm a painter myself."

I somehow mollified Ratanlal when, in addition to the pizza he ordered an expensive ice cream as well.

Then many years later I got a phone call from Ratanlal: "I want to show you two Souzas and you have to give me your absolutely frank opinion. I think they are genuine."

"Where did you get them?"

"A guy brought them from Patna."

"Where is he staying?"

"Chittaranjan Park."

"Then they are fake."

"Why? Why do you say that? Top galleries deal with this guy. If I were to tell you their names you'd lose your sleep."

"When did I say that top galleries don't sell fakes. That guy has come from Kolkata not Patna. These rackets of fake painting are well-known. Chintan Upadhyaya once rushed to Kolkata from Mumbai the moment he heard that his works were being copied there. He also said with a laugh that if the copier was a good artist he'd make him his assistant."

"Chintan has suffered injustice. Look, he is still behind bars."

"That's a different question. Even I sympathise with him. But why do you want to show the Souzas to me? I consider myself a Souza disciple just as Eklavya considered Dronacharya his guru. How can I authenticate his paintings? What is my standing? You better approach his daughter Shelley in New York."

"But she doesn't even answer the mail."

"Well, hard cash can do anything. I've heard Souza's son once terrorised Shelley. You might know she is the only daughter of Souza's first wife. The son is from his second wife and has his own issues."

"Actually I phoned you because you are quite close to Mathur. He listens to you. He has also written a fat book on Souza. A certificate from him will convince my buyer."

"But he no longer picks up my phone. Anyway, why don't you come with me? I'm coming to your house in a taxi. I have a bottle of expensive liquor. Let's go to Mathur's den with the paintings."

"Is it a Blue Label?"

"That's a good joke. I've somehow managed even a Black Label with great difficulty."

"What if Mathur is not at home?"

"He *will* be. I've checked on the landline."

"It's evening now. If he has a lady disciple with him he'd be very cross."

"Arre bhai, try to understand. If he finds the paintings are genuine, then the works would fetch him 5 lakhs each and you'd also make a lakh each. Mathur has to just give the green signal."

Mathur was delighted to see the Black Label. He had a rather cheap brand on his table and was about to pour his first peg when we landed. The presence of a lady disciple was a given. She was doing research in Benares on the new trends in abstract art. But she hadn't come alone. She was newly-married and her husband was in the army who knew zilch about the world of art. Her name was Sulochana and she was one of those friends of mine who take no time in clicking 'Like' on the Facebook. Facebook would be a desolate place but for such friends.

Before opening the bottle, Ratanlal unwrapped the two so-called Souzas and put them up on display in the room. One was a 1961 landscape, the other a contorted face made in the 1980s.

Mathur kept quiet, just silently checked out the paintings. Then he made a large peg for himself out of the Black Label (a Patiala peg would have looked small in comparison!), downed it neat in one go and said: "If you want to enjoy Black Label, never pour water in it."

Sulochana tried to get up: "Sir, I better leave. It's getting late."

"Arre bhai, let your husband have at least one peg. We have bored him enough discussing Kandinsky and Gaitonde. Being in the army he must be drinking."

Without caring to look at Sulochana, her husband quickly poured a large peg for himself and said: "Cheers."

Sulochana didn't like that. She messaged me on Messenger: "Look at my husband. An idiot. I had told him to go to his army club but he's clinging on to me, mistrusting even an elderly gentleman like Mathur Saheb."

My quick riposte was: "Mathur is not an elderly gentleman. He is a bastard No. 1 and your husband won't leave you alone today."

She said: "I'm having periods."

"At such times the desire becomes more intense."

"No. It becomes something abstract."

She began to laugh and so did I. Sulochana's husband suddenly turned quite pally with Mathur and quickly poured another peg.

Ratanlal now became jittery.

Mathur could sense he was uneasy and got up to see the paintings up close, then returned to his chair. "Yaar Jai, it's quite strange. You down a large peg and then you begin to feel these paintings are actually by Souza."

"Keep them here overnight. Maybe by morning you'd find they're 100 per cent genuine."

"No, I can't take that risk. Mice still romp about the house and if they nibble away your priceless paintings what will I do?"

Even Ratanlal began to laugh.

I now noticed a lizard on the wall. It flitted about just behind Mathur and I warned him.

"I fear nothing, only the Tihar Jail scares me. I've had this dreadful dream time and again that I've been locked up in Tihar for certifying a fake Husain as genuine and a fat mouse is romping around me and I'm in deep shit."

It was obvious his one peg had been rather extraordinarily large.

Sulochana was quite annoyed that her husband had poured yet another peg for himself. She quickly picked up her empty glass of water, made a neat peg and downed it.

I messaged her: "Bravo! That was the right thing to do. Why not make another one."

She did, when her husband suddenly remembered the army discipline, stood up and both of them took leave. But all through the night Sulochana continued to barrage me with her 'bold' messages. There is something called phone sex but there is also a genre called Messenger sex.

Ratanlal sat there drinking like a very disciplined man. Then he asked Mathur: "So would you certify them? You'll get five lakh for each painting. All in cash."

"Arre bhai, who am I to certify Souza? Fine, I've written a book on him. I also have a lot of his letters. But what is my stature?"

"Arre sir, the buyers are ready to snap them. All I need is your certificate."

"Then do one thing. Tomorrow, show these paintings to the buyer again. If he is really willing to pay your price then come to me and I'd give in writing that keeping in view whatever I know, these paintings are genuine."

Ratanlal was delighted. He packed the paintings and prepared to take leave: "I'll phone you tomorrow."

"All right."

Afterwards, Mathur confided: "Let me see which cashbull is fooled by him. Nobody's going to buy them. This skunk is not going to lay hands on 80 lakhs or 60 lakhs just like that."

This roused in me a wee bit of respect for Mathur; after all he hadn't sold himself out completely.

The following afternoon, on leaving the Central Secretariat metro station, as I walked towards India Gate, I noticed a crowd gathered around a luxury car. A policeman was also there. Evidently the car had hit a boy who had suffered some minor bruises. As I reached the spot I noticed the car owner was Sunil, the only son of the art world's latest international discovery Roop Narayan.

The policeman was suggesting that Sunil give the boy some cash so he could have himself bandaged. Sunil's argument was that he had purposefully jumped in front of his car to make easy money and that such boys operated in gangs and pretended to have been hurt by luxury car owners. I calmed Sunil down, asked him to pay the boy 2,000 rupees and close the matter.

"These bastards are gangsters." Sunil was quite incensed. Then insisted: "Yaar, we are meeting after a long time. Come, let me show you my new flat. It's not very far from Khan Market."

I didn't tell Sunil but I could see in the distance the policeman taking from the boy half his share of the loot.

Sunil was around 40, the son of a big dad. And lately the big dad had become even bigger. I would often quote to Sunil, if only to tease him, a line from a poem I had read somewhere: 'I'm the son of a mighty bird/ Lounging on a sofa since arriving in the world'.

Sunil had completed his higher studies in art in America though he was just an average student at Delhi College. But his father's cash opened many doors for him. On his return to India he lost his focus on account of the New Art. The man-made creditable paintings on the canvas but once the installation bug bit him he virtually stopped painting.

"Painting is something outdated now," he would declare proudly. He had rented the ground floor of the large gallery at Rabindra Bhavan and put up a huge installation there. On the day the show was inaugurated, the Press could be seen tailing his famous father Roop Narayan the moment he arrived. One of his paintings had sold for 5 crores just a couple of days earlier at a London auction.

Until a years ago Sunil would get bugged by the very mention of his father's name. Sometimes I would on purpose call him Sunil Roop Narayan when he would fly off the handle.

"This big dad's name has become a problem for me. I am Sunil – just Sunil."

And now when I arrived at his third-floor flat near Khan Market in a lift, the nameplate at the door surprised me – '*Sunil Roop Narayan*'.

A servant opened the door. I was surprised and said: "Abe Sunil, what am I seeing? How did you become Sunil Roop Narayan? The very mention of this name would make you furious and now you have proudly put up a nameplate with those words."

He didn't react. He was in a hurry to reach the bar. "That boy made me so furious."

"Abe, your dad is all over the town nowadays."

Sunil remained silent for a while.

"Whatever you say, Roop Narayanji is extremely lucky. Even in his old age he is surrounded by beautiful women. On his 80th birthday party at Maurya Hotel he announced out of the blue that he would sign his posters only for the women present at the party. And lo! The media found the *masala* when the women, all dressed up to their nines for the party, queued up in front of him. At that point a clown among the Pressmen went up to Roop Narayan, busy signing the posters, and said: "Sir, I know you won't sign my poster. So I'm not joining the queue."

Roop Narayan smiled, took two posters from his hand, signed them and on one also drew a lovely sparrow. Then chuckled: "Continuing to remain in the news is an art. This queue of lovely ladies is only for the sake of the media."

"The old man's only problem is women," Sunil said.

"Yaar, at least learn to respect your dad. Even this flat was given to him by a builder in return for a painting."

"But that bastard was absolutely unwilling to buy my installation at the show. Told me that he couldn't make out my art."

"These guys aren't collectors if you ask me. They are builders. All the same the art world is running thanks only to their generosity."

"As for my dad, he is a strange character. One day he called me from New York in the early morning. Asked me what I was up to. 'Are you drinking?' I said, 'No dad. I'm with my girlfriend and she doesn't like to drink.' He said, 'You are doing the right thing. Let me speak to her.' And my girlfriend was busy talking to my dad for half an hour."

These days, in every photograph in the media Roop Narayan was to be seen in the company of a society beauty who went by the name of Kamini Jaiswal. Her husband was a well-known lawyer. Both her kids were studying abroad and the lawyer hardly had time to spare from his practice. What made him happy was the sight of his wife's pictures in newspapers standing next to a famous painter. A couple of times even his own photograph appeared in print: 'Roop Narayan, his companion and another friend'.

The lawyer's hard work was falling short of allowing him to make a move from Greater Kailash to Golf Links but the speed with which Roop Narayan showered the gifts of paintings on Kamini finally fulfilled their dream of owning a house in the posh colony.

"After 20 years the wife begins to look like a sister," he would proudly tell his friends between whiffs on a pipe.

But that day Sunil was merciless and said: "Don't talk about that bitch. She's a prostitute. She's looting my dad openly."

I didn't agree there. Fine, Kamini was benefiting big time thanks to Roop Narayan's bounties. But she herself wrote fine poetry, would speak about painting quite sensibly and her personality and mode of conversation matched Roop Narayan's in every respect.

"Yaar, Kamini is a very sophisticated woman. Don't call her a prostitute."

"You don't know how my mother has to lead a lonely life in her palatial house."

"But Roop Narayan didn't walk out on her."

At a charity auction at the Gymkhana Club once, Kamini had included one of my paintings too. Roop Narayan too had once given me the 'Master Artist of Tomorrow' award which was overseen by Kamini. She said to me at the time : "Come home sometimes."

"Yes, I'd surely come. I've heard you have a very large collection of Roop Naraynaji's works. I would certainly like to see it."

"Arre bhai, there is much else at my place. I not only write poetry, but paint as well. There was a time I also played sitar on the stage."

"Roop Narayanji's 'Sitar Vadika' is an amazing painting. The magical spread of open hair, the sitar and you…"

Kamini's charming personality would attract anyone. When I arrived at her home her lawyer husband himself brought over the beer in a tray and was quite polite and deferential. That the country's one of the leading artists was smitten by his wife was also a matter of pride for him.

Kamini kept me busy for a long time showing her collection. She had at least 20 to 22 expensive paintings by Roop Narayan. A nude with her hair untied, which hung in the bedroom, was arresting. I continued to contemplate it for a long while.

"What are you looking at my child? Looks like the nude has fascinated you."

I used to be quite shy in those days.

"Don't feel bad but it looks like you are the model."

"What's there to feel bad about? There is a divine pleasure in becoming a great artist's muse."

"Doesn't Vakil Saheb feel odd?"

Even her laughter was quite heady. She couldn't stop laughing for quite a while. "If he did, would this painting have a place of pride in our bedroom?"

Just then Vakil Saheb entered with another can of beer.

"Vakil Saheb is a thorough gentleman!" I said once he had left.

"Yes, I'm very lucky. I met only good men in my life. Though I don't think you are one of them."

"Then am I a rogue Kaminiji?"

"Well, you look like one. The way you were leering at the nude."

"Kaminiji, may I use your bathroom?

"Shouldn't have too much beer otherwise you'd grow a beer belly like Vakil Saheb."

"No, I mean to do something naughty. I'm unable to control myself."

"If you dirty my bathroom I'd thrash you. I don't know why today's boys don't want to hide anything. Is anyone asking you what you are going to do in there?"

Though I hardly take selfies, before going into the bathroom I did take a nice one with Kamini, recalling a Souza drawing where a devil stands next to a beauty.

Roop Narayan had studios in many cities, including one next to Piazza Navonna in Rome. I visited him even there once.

Roop Narayan had told me on the phone: "I've been painting since 5 in the morning. It's a large work for Venice Biennale. You'd see it when you come."

I didn't know that Kamini was also in Rome. When I landed in his studio, Roop Narayan was giving finishing touches to an amazing painting on a large canvas. If colours trickled on the floor Kamini would very gently wipe them with a piece of cloth. She had just come out of her bathroom, her hair still wet.

It's unfair for Sunil to call Kamini a prostitute. The children believe that in their old age their dads should only concern themselves with religion and spirituality and should retire. In any case I felt Sunil looked far older than his father – a dreary drunkard.

Chapter 10

THE NIGHT BUS AT 11

In the early morning I got this phone call from Sunil. He was quite excited: "Arre Jai, I saw on Facebook this report that there's a law whereby an artist's family is entitled to a percentage of the royalty on the resale of his work. Surprisingly, nobody has noticed this 1994 copyright law."

"I can see it's natural for you to be delighted. In this case you and your dad can claim a lot of royalty."

"You seem to restrict an issue to a small circuit and that's the end of it for you. Actually, it's an issue which can benefit even you at some stage. The question covers the entire art fraternity. But is any prominent artist's family aware of the details or legal implications of this subject? We need to come together to understand and examine it."

"Come, let's hold a rally in front of the Parliament next week. I'm ready and you'd also be prepared. But watch out, your dad is not going to raise slogans standing in the front row."

"You don't know my father. He'd be prepared to do anything absurd just to be in the news."

"Well, you have a great opinion about your dad."

"One can be a great artist but not necessarily a great father, husband or brother."

"Now that you are talking about the royalty and the resale, I'm sure you also know that many artists' family members issue authenticity certificates of their fake paintings when they are offered good sums for the service. And sometimes an eminent artist himself declines to issue a certificate for some very old work of his though he knows very well it's authentic. Even an artist of the stature of Padamsee has said that if one wants his authentic work he should buy it from him directly. 'The galleries are selling a lot of my fakes', he says. But when an artist is young, galleries alone promote his work. And gradually their prices also begin to rise."

"Yaar, you tend to go too deeply into an issue. Even I realise the entire issue is quite complicated."

"When Tyeb Mehta's 'Kali' goes for more than 26 crores at an auction the art world does take notice. Remember the time when an NRI bought a Tyeb Mehta for 7 crores and made people sit up? A film-maker told me that in 1996 he had gone to interview Tyeb Mehta at his tiny flat in Juhu where he saw in a corner of his small bedroom a painting lying on an easel. He was seriously ill at the time. But after the 7-crore magic he did manage to have a good time at least for a short while. Van Gogh, the artist to fetch the highest price in the world, could sell only one work in all his depressing life. And consider Modigliani's tragic life. An art dealer was negotiating to buy all his works even as he lay on the deathbed."

"Yaar, let's meet in a bar. You seem to have a treasure trove of useful information."

"And you have your dad's stuff. Why don't you say that?"

"Dad splurges his fortune on his begum! And I also get to have some dole."

"Why? Doesn't your dad have the right to enjoy to the full the few remaining years of his life? Why must children alone have the sole right on their father's fortune? You have so much and you still seem unhappy. The woman you call a prostitute is your great father's goddess of art – his muse."

"But a prostitute is a prostitute. Why do you sanctify her as a goddess of art? If you had your way even you would try to seduce her. You pry into her bedroom and then go into her bathroom…"

"It's a mistake to share anything with you. Fine, go and post my love for her on Facebook. Tell everyone that I was staring at her nude made by your great father."

I put the phone down. Arguing with Sunil was a waste of time. He had become irrelevant as an artist and his father's wealth alone was his mainstay, the father he once hated and didn't even want his own name to be associated with his.

"Fuck off!" I screamed, alone in my house. I'm not a Rajneesh follower but I was amused to see somewhere a video of his discourse on the word 'fuck' and many of its meanings and contexts. According to Rajneesh the English word 'fuck' is quite magical. Its sound connotes both pain and pleasure, hatred and love.

The Hindi language doesn't have any magical word like it with such a wide a range of meanings and contexts. In American movies it is well-nigh impossible to complete a sentence without the word 'fuck'. When a poor and defenceless viewer does nowadays get to hear a word like '*chodna*' in Anurag Kashyap's movies, he still fails to conjure up or hear the natural sound the word 'fuck' emanates.

Even so, God knows why, even today if a girl lying on the bed says 'fuck me' that hardly has any effect on me. But if she says 'Mujhe chod do' that expression sounds so very magical and exciting.

I was once telling about my theory to my old classmate Mithilesh who was counted among the most brilliant students in the college. But no sooner had she got the degree when she married a bank employee under pressure from her family. Since he was in the Cash Department, he had this habit of always trying to count the notes.

"I'm sure you've seen Chaplin's movie *Modern Times* . In it, Chaplin works in a factory where he has to tighten the screws all day. But after tightening the screws for hours on end one day he reaches the point where, when he notices a woman wearing a dress with black buttons he runs towards her to tighten them in the misguided belief they are screws. Similarly, my husband can be seen counting notes in the bed even in his most intimate moments. I got sick of it one day and told him that now that counting machines had arrived, he better give up the disturbing habit."

"When I hear your stories, I sometimes feel I did well by not getting married."

"Perhaps it's better for a woman artist to marry a male artist otherwise take it that your career is over."

Mithilesh was in a good mood. That evening there was this birthday party of our old friend Raghav's wife Priya. Both were artists. The wife worked in a school and the husband freelanced. Their life ran on an even keel. Raghav also took care of their two children and seemed happy with the responsibility.

"Yaar Jai, I've also been invited to the birthday party. And I also feel like having a couple of pegs. But the boring Cash Department at home would leave me sober by his repeated phone calls."

"Just don't take them. Make some excuse. I think it's a good opportunity to meet old friends. In any case my life nowadays is going through a big drought."

Mithilesh finally decided to join the party. To hell with the Cash Department. On arriving at Priya's house, she asked her: "Just phone my husband on this number and tell him that you had pressed me to stay back for the party."

"Yaar, I have to prepare the chicken. Why don't you tell Raghav to phone him?"

"You are not following yaar. My husband is a distrustful type. If *you* phone him, he'd think it's a ladies' party."

Priya smiled and told Mithilesh's husband quite warmly: "Please do come to my birthday party. Bring along the kids too. It's a ladies' party but some husbands can also come. You'd really enjoy the fare at our party of artists."

Mithilesh knew her husband wouldn't turn up. And she didn't want him to come either, only to spoil the party and take the fun out of it. On top of that, he'd have to have his peg mixed with Coke. Mithilesh didn't want the evening spoilt and was keen to have some fleeting moments of joy for herself.

But her husband continued to phone every 15 to 20 minutes. Mithilesh finally switched her phone off but her husband was hardly deterred. He now began to phone Priya until a harried Priya told him: "Bhai Saheb, please don't feel bad. But if in the middle of talking to you I mistakenly pour some extra rum into the chicken then its taste will go. Wouldn't it be better if you joined the party with your kids."

There was no call from Mithilesh's Cash Department after this. She told Priya: "Now he'd be even more worried, wondering whether the rum was being poured only in the chicken or into his wife's Coke as well."

By now the party was in full swing. The topic of the evening was why must an artist marry only an artist.

I gave a new twist to the subject: "A couple of days ago I was watching at Dhoomimal Gallery a video of senior artist Arpita Singh's conversation. In it she says at one point that 'When I was studying in the arts college in the 1950s, every day I would hear people say they took the 11pm bus home. All male artists would hang out in Connaught Place after spending the evening at the Coffee House. The last bus left at 11.' Arpitaji's mother had strict instructions she must be back home by nightfall. We are not talking about today. Imagine the milieu 60 years ago. Arpitaji said: 'I married a painter so I could also take the 11 o'clock bus.'"

"Arpitaji said something very significant!" said Raghav. "We boys are never able to follow it. We notice a girl holding a cigarette or a glass of liquor and it makes us heady. And if a single girl decides to catch an 11 o'clock bus in a city like Delhi today, you can imagine the real terror in her heart."

The discussion was going on well when Mithilesh had to leave the party midway. Her husband was waiting downstairs on his scooter, calling Priya time and time again on the phone.

Mithilesh called me after two days. "I have written a statement about myself and my art for a group show catalogue. Have sent it just now on WhasApp. I want your sincere advice. If you find the language is a bit shaky sort it out."

"Did your Cash Department sniff you that day or not?"

"I told him 'If you try to sniff me today I'd thrash you. I had to leave in the middle of the party only because of you.'"

I read Mithilesh's statement carefully. She had written about her art quite honestly but the last line was not honest. She wrote: 'My parents have contributed a lot in enabling me to reach these heights in the art world and my husband has also supported me always. I'm particularly grateful to him'.

"Was it necessary to give a false certificate to your husband? Delete that line!"

"What difference does it make? If I only talk about my parents' contribution he'd make my life difficult. I have to bear with this animal all my life. But if you can give me space in your studio, I can leave him for good and come over."

"If you start to live in my studio your husband will go on a fast unto death at my doorstep."

Mithilesh couldn't help laughing.

"I sometimes have this feeling I've been worshipping this ass for no reason. I'm an artist and still not free." She began to whimper now.

I understood what was going on in her mind. The world of painting has strange rules. You have to reach the point of insanity and yet make sure you don't go mad. The spirit of gay abandon is essential for an artist but the madness needs to have a method too.

But I have also witnessed and known closely a rebel artist who lived all her life on her own terms but after crossing 50 acquiesced to become the companion of a senior artist who wanted to entirely delete her past from her biodata. And yet the rebel artist didn't see anything wrong in that.

That rebel artist was Devyani. She was a guest lecturer in our college. When I was a first-year student, Devyani's very first lecture floored me. She had entered the class smoking a cigarette and then stubbed it after saying 'Oh'. I was drawn not only to her personality but was highly impressed by her intellectual reach as well.

After the class everyone was talking only about her. It was our first day in the college and all the students were new. Since morning we'd been listening to the discourses of dull and boring lecturers. Devyani's entry into this insipid atmosphere was like a strong gust of fresh air.

As soon as she left the class, Neeraj said: "Devyani ma'am created a storm in the Press when she put up a show of her male nudes in

Mumbai last year. She gave many TV interviews as well. She is a very cool painter. Even men are afraid of her."

One evening, as I sat enjoying hot samosas and tea at Mandi House, I spotted Devyani. She was also having tea there. She had just watched a play and was abusing the director mercilessly.

One noticeable thing about Devyani ma'am (surely she was our ma'am in those days) was that when talking to her students she wouldn't impose her lecturer's persona on them. She was quite natural and would interact like a friend.

"Ma'am, I've heard your show of male nudes had created a flutter in Mumbai."

Devyani had a peculiar sort of laughter. She said: "So have you decided to become a model for me? I can take you on but won't pay you anything."

"No, not really. I was merely inquiring. I don't have a model's body."

"Now listen to this interesting story. Balbhadra Agrawal is a big Delhi businessman. And he likes nudes. And Virendra Bhatia is supposed to be the master of painting nudes. Agrawal had been buying his nudes for many years though his wife was always quite annoyed with this passion of her middle-aged husband. One day he called me over, showed me his collection, and said please paint some nudes for me. I told him I only painted male nudes. But he was insistent, claiming he was quite impressed by my skill and then said: 'Please make some female nudes too for my sake'. I didn't agree."

"Why only male nudes?"

"Because the history of art worldwide is replete with images of female nudes. I make nudes of ordinary people, not of Greek gods."

One day Mathur narrated to me Devyani's life story, making it a bit spicy in the process. She was from Bareilly where she had fallen in love with her handsome teacher and after only 15 days of courtship gone ahead and married him. In a town like Bareilly the news of someone marrying her teacher would be something quite scandalous. The teacher now wanted to make sure his wife's talent won't run to seed in that small town. So for further studies he sent Devyani to a prestigious arts university in Vadodara. Once there, she came in contact with an intellectual lecturer, decided to seek divorce from her husband and then not marry anyone. Instead, like those who change their cultural kurtas of FabIndia every six months, Devyani fell into the pattern of changing her male friends.

After listening to her story, I began to look for ways to take my friendship with Devyani forward. One day I landed up at her studio unannounced.

"What brings you here?"

"Nothing ma'am, I was in the neighbourhood so thought I should take a peek at your studio."

We had a long discussion starting out with Herbert Read and moved on to John Berger.

Devyani was chain-smoking. Then out of the blue she told me: "By the way you can still become my nude model. I don't look for a perfect body."

"Ma'am it's a very difficult task. You may ask me to do anything else."

"No, you look like the right model for my painting. Bloody men take no time in going naked in front of a woman, taking off their trousers in a jiffy."

"Yes, but I'm not that kind of a man."

"Why don't you look into my eyes and talk? Your shifting eyes tell me that you are suffering from some kind of an inferiority complex."

I now tried to look into Devyani's eyes. She was my teacher. She was senior to me in age but her style was maddening and it took me no time to take off my clothes. Indeed she was senior to me by many years. But even in bed her actions were rather innovative. At least for me they were.

"I'm a born rebel, Jai Kumar."

Next time in the class I wouldn't take my eyes off Devyani. All of us were to draw portraits. I made quite a charming one of Devyani with a romantic flourish.

She came over to me and looked on as I worked. Then told me: "This romance-vomance won't do young man! You better struggle a bit with the life's realities. Spend an entire day at the Old Delhi railway station tomorrow. Look at the ordinary folk, the coolies shedding their sweat. Draw their portraits. The age of romantic portraiture is over."

I spent the following day actually sketching in a non-romantic style the passengers and the coolies at the huge Old Delhi platform. At the end of it my sketch-book had no space left. I had laboured under the spell of some intense creative hysteria.

Devyani phoned me at 7 in the evening: "Young man, I didn't see you in the class today. Were you upset with what I told you?"

"No ma'am, I was at the Old Delhi station with my sketch-book since morning. And I found some amazing faces. You were right. The age of romance is over."

"Then come down to my studio with your sketch-book. Let me see your master-strokes."

That's exactly what I was looking for. That night I had to sleep over at her studio. My sketches had impressed her highly. And I went crazy about her man-eating manoeuvres, enjoying the experience of having Marilyn Monroe, Mata Hari, Rani of Jhansi and Rosa Luxemburg all at once in my arms. I recalled that poem by Dhoomil: *As I lay next to that woman I realised / Going naked is a strong move against blindness.*

I agreed to become Devyani's model and she made my nude sketches over a number of days. She had already booked the Shridharani Gallery. The show was titled 'Doors of Passion'.

"Ma'am, everybody will recognise me. I'd be in a difficult situation. And it might hurt your reputation as well. After all I'm your student."

"To hell with reputation. You're getting scared for nothing. I do what I like. When my teacher could marry me, then my student also can do anything."

"So are you going to marry me?"

Devyani puffed at a cigarette and smiled. Then said: "Marriage lines have disappeared from my hand."

Obviously, the show got a very good coverage in the Press. On the day of the inauguration the TV guys asked Devyani right there in front of the audience: "Is your model really one of your students?"

Devyani's reply was quite bold: "One can find inspiration anywhere. Let's talk about these paintings. Talk about what is the strength or weakness of my art. Whether my model is my student or my laundryman is of no consequence."

By the time the show concluded the principal had sacked Devyani. That was hardly a problem for her since she was a guest lecturer anyway. Soon after, Devyani left for Paris for a year on scholarship.

But now in 2018 God knows where the rebellious streak in Devyani has disappeared. She discovered Sohanlal, a senior artist, as she entered her middle age. Now one hardly sees her step out of her house. She still paints, and her shows are still held. But she doesn't go even for their inauguration. It was after considerable persuasion that she consented to have a documentary made on her art. But Sohanlal warned the director beforehand: "Devyani has no past. You don't have to talk about her past life at all. Even the name of her previous husband must not be mentioned in her bio-data.

I couldn't bear the sight of a born rebel ending up in this situation.

Chapter 11

KHUSHI ARRIVES AND DEPARTS

I do not like the month of August in Delhi. For one, the security arrangements in view of August 15 celebrations continue to cause a lot of inconvenience. Second, the rainy season nowadays brings along so many epidemics in its wake that it hardly leaves any scope for romantic fantasies. There was a time when October was counted among the most glorious in Delhi – the best month in the year. But today you have to cross the depressing maze of all those ailments before reaching October and by then you have no energy left.

I have been sick since the first day of August and it's 11th today. Am I going to be down with a dangerous bout of dengue? I have no appetite left, haven't opened a bottle for many days and don't feel like musing over my happy memories either.

But thc weather has improved a bit since morning. It's been drizzling. I have been wanting to enjoy this rare sight standing in the balcony, but my heart is not there.

Suddenly the doorbell rings. Someone is pressing it hard. Is the godforsaken guy some new cleaner in the area?

There stands a woman in her early forties in a beautiful sari. With her is an attractive, dusky girl, about 18 or 19, in a particoloured suit.

"Do you know me? I am Khushi. Your Khushi. I'm sure you recognise my voice. You've been hearing it for a long time. Today I thought, let me also go. She is Jaya. A newcomer in my group."

"You should have phoned at least."

"I wanted to give you a surprise. Doesn't happiness come as a surprise after all?"

"Even so you should have phoned before coming. Generally, I'm not at home."

"Painter Babu, make a portrait of Khushi too please. I've never asked you for anything."

I took out my Canon camera and, with the rain in the background, clicked some 20 or 25 photos of Jaya as she stood in the balcony. Her face was quite cinematic.

"What do you do?"

"Nothing. Just sit at home."

"Who are the people at home?"

"My husband. He's a driver."

"You are married already?"

Khushi told me she was 19, her grandparents lived in Tamil Nadu, Herfather had been a rickshaw puller in Delhi for many years and that she was born in Delhi itself and spoke Hindi fluently.

Jaya quite shyly whispered something in Khushi's ears.

"What is she telling you?"

"She's praising you. Says ever since she's entered this profession everyone wants to photograph her only in the nude. You are the first man who has snapped her in clothes."

"Where do *you* come from Khushi?"

"I'm from Maharashtra."

"But Mathur told me you are from Bangladesh."

"Well, my husband is a Marathi. So now am I not a Marathi too?"

"Shall I make your portrait?" I asked her. I hadn't even touched my brush for a long time.

"Oh my God. That's exactly what I want."

I quickly made her portrait. It was a good one. I felt the artist in me hadn't yet died.

Khushi was highly excited. "May I take it?" she asked. "I'll have it framed."

"Of course. It's for you only."

I went in and began to look for some cash and finally found a 2000-rupee note. I felt relieved, came out and handed it to Khushi.

"I'll prepare fish today. If you allow me, I can make very delicious fish for you too."

"Yes, why not. But these days I don't feel like eating anything."

Khushi nudged Jaya. "Go and make Saheb happy. He's a thorough gentleman. I'd sit here and watch TV."

"No, no. I'm not in a mood today."

"Sir, at least go and look at her. She's a very good girl. Everybody praises her."

"No, not today. Give a thousand to Jaya. She should get a nice suit for herself. Then I'll take more of her photos."

Jaya had a beatific smile. She stepped forward and embraced me.

Now Khushi began to complain: "The security man at the gate of your colony harasses a lot. Asks a lot of odd questions. What brings you here… why have you come..."

"I'll phone him. Then he won't say anything though he might question you on seeing the painting in your hand."

I watched Khushi and Jaya as they walked past my balcony. Jaya turned back, looked up at me and waved in excitement. And I found myself waving back to both Jaya and Khushi with all the enthusiasm I could muster, like a child bidding goodbye to unknown passengers in a moving train.

But has Khushi really departed?

FINISH